If you have a home computer with Internet access you may:
- request an item to be placed on hold.
- renew an item that is not overdue or on hold.
- view titles and due dates checked out on your card.
- view and/or pay your outstanding fines online (over $5).

To view your patron record from your home computer click on Patchogue-Medford Library's homepage:  www.pmlib.org

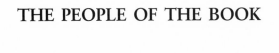

THE PEOPLE OF THE BOOK

THE PEOPLE

of

THE BOOK

PHILOSEMITISM IN ENGLAND, FROM CROMWELL TO CHURCHILL

Gertrude Himmelfarb

ENCOUNTER BOOKS *e* NEW YORK • LONDON

First American edition published in 2011 by Encounter Books, an activity of Encounter for Culture and Education, Inc., a nonprofit, tax exempt corporation. Encounter Books website address: www.encounterbooks.com

Manufactured in the United States and printed on acid-free paper. The paper used in this publication meets the minimum requirements of ANSI/NISO Z39.48-1992 (R 1997) (*Permanence of Paper*).

FIRST AMERICAN EDITION

LIBRARY OF CONGRESS CATALOGING-IN-PUBLICATION DATA
Himmelfarb, Gertrude.
The people of the book: philosemitism in England, from Cromwell to Churchill/by Gertrude Himmelfarb.
p. cm.
Includes bibliographical references and index.
ISBN-13: 978-1-59403-570-8 (hardcover: alk. paper)
ISBN-10: 1-59403-570-9 (hardcover: alk. paper) 1. Jews—Great Britain—History—17th century. 2. Philosemitism—Great Britain. 3. Great Britain—Intellectual life—17th century. 4. Great Britain—Politics and government—1603–1714. 5. Great Britain—Ethnic relations. I. Title. II. Title: Philosemitism in England, from Cromwell to Churchill.
DS135.E5H56 2011
305.892'40420903—dc22

2011013351

10 9 8 7 6 5 4 3 2 1

In memory of my husband, Irving Kristol

Contents

Prologue

The scholarly literature on antisemitism is voluminous, reflecting the painstaking attempts by historians to recover and recount the long and horrendous history of antisemitism. The literature on philosemitism, on the other hand, reflecting a favorable view of Jews, is meager, not only because the evidence is slighter and less dramatic than antisemitism but also because it does not challenge the imagination or the indignation of scholars. The discrepancy between the two is understandable but unfortunate, for it reduces Judaism to the eternal recurrence of persecution and the struggle for survival. It also has the effect of debasing Jews, "objectifying" them, making them not subjects in their own right but the objects, if not of hatred and contempt, then of pity and pathos.

Shortly after the end of World War II, the French philosopher Jean-Paul Sartre published *Réflexions sur la question juive*, retitled, for the English edition, *Anti-Semite and Jew*. It is there that he coined the much-quoted aphorism: "It is not the Jewish character that provokes antisemitism. It is the antisemite who creates the Jew." He then proposed, as the "necessary and sufficient" solution to "the Jewish question," a socialist revolution that would finally eliminate antisemitism.[1] That solution has long since been discredited. But what has persisted is the image of the Jew as the perennial victim and martyr, of Judaism as an outmoded and discredited creed, and of Israel as the refuge of harried Jews seeking asylum from prejudice, oppression, and, possibly, another Holocaust.

It is not only non-Jews who have this image of Jews. Nor is it a recent phenomenon, an all-too-plausible response to the Holocaust. It was in 1928 that a young Jewish historian, Salo Baron, a recent immigrant to America from Austria, wrote an article in the *Menorah Journal* deploring the "lachrymose theory" of Jewish history which had been perpetuated by the eminent nineteenth-century German-Jewish scholar Heinrich Graetz.[2] That article was written well before the Holocaust, but Baron, who went on to write a massive history of the Jews, persisted in his critique of that view of Jewish history—in spite of the fact that his own parents were killed in the Holocaust.

For other Jews, however, seared by the experience and the memory of Nazism, the Holocaust has become the defining event, not only of modern Jewish history but of Judaism itself. The philosopher and rabbi Emil Fackenheim, himself a refugee from Nazi Germany (having escaped from a concentration camp), gave memorable expression to this view in his creation of a "614th Commandment," supplementing the traditional 613 *mitzvot* binding on Jews. The new commandment enjoins Jews to remain Jews lest they give a posthumous victory to Hitler.[3] This is a dramatic dictum reflecting a deeply moving sentiment. It has, however, the unwitting effect of giving Hitler precisely that posthumous victory by permitting him to intrude into the venerable declaration of faith.

A history of philosemitism may help counteract this "lach-rymose" view of Jewish history. This is not to deny or belittle the history of antisemitism, which reached its apogee in the Holocaust, but rather to complement it by revealing another aspect of Jewish experience—the respect, even reverence, for Jews and Judaism displayed by non-Jews before and after the Holocaust. This new history, a counter-history, so to speak, is needed now more than ever, to put in perspective the recent resurgence of antisemitism throughout the world, which has produced, in turn, a formidably scholarly literature on the history of antisemitism. It was the request I received within a week or so from different journals to review three such histories, published within months of each other, that prompted me to undertake this study.[4] Surely, I felt, Judaism is more than the history of antisemitism. Surely Jews deserve to be defined—and are in fact defined, by others as well as by themselves—by those qualities of faith, lineage, sacred texts, and moral teachings that have enabled them to endure through centuries of persecution.

The resurgence of antisemitism is most ominous in England because it is so discordant, so out of keeping with the spirit of the country. In 1999, the final chapter of a book on philosemitism in the English-speaking world opened with the comforting assertion that where antisemitism was once the norm and philosemitism the exception, now the situation has been reversed; philosemitism is now the norm and antisemitism the exception. "Indeed, antisemitism in the mainstream has declined to such an extent that it has virtually disappeared, or may well be seen as on the way to disappearance within a generation or two."[5] Less than ten years later, the same historian published a book with the ominous subtitle "The Fall and Rise of Antisemitism."[6] More recently, another historian, introducing a massive history of antisemitism in England, observes that "philosemitism, as an aspect of public discourse, did not survive the passing of the twentieth century." It is now England's "past glory."[7]

That conclusion may be overly pessimistic. In any case, a history of philosemitism may well start with England, which, more than any other country, has produced, over the past several centuries, a rich literature of philosemitism, reflecting the principles and policies that have made modern England a model of liberality and civility.[*]

The word "philosemitism," however, has its difficulties. Applied to earlier periods of history, it is, strictly speaking, an anachronism. But so is "antisemitism." Both words originated in Germany about the same time. *Antisemitismus* appeared in 1879 in a book by Wilhelm Marr, *Der Weg zum Siege des Germantums über des Judentums* (*The Way to Victory of Germanism over Judaism*), and in the title of the organization he founded, the League of Antisemites. The following year the highly regarded (and avowedly antisemitic) historian Heinrich von Treitschke, in a speech in the Chamber of Deputies, referred contemptuously to the "blind philosemitic zeal of the party of progress"—"Jew-lovers," one might say, who sympathized with the Jews during the recent wave of attacks on them in Germany. (Treitschke also has the distinction of having coined the phrase, later adopted by the Nazi journal *Der Stürmer* as its motto, "*Die Juden sind unser Unglück*"—"The Jews are our misfortune").[8] The word "philosemitism" was soon picked up by other German antisemites in the same derogatory sense. Thus both words, antisemitism and philosemitism, were invented in Germany by antisemites—antisemitism used approvingly, philosemitism disparagingly.

---

* I speak of "England," rather than "Britain," partly because a good deal of this story is about England before it became Britain, but also because that is the term contemporaries generally used even for the later period, as many of the quotations in the following chapters and the titles of books on the subject testify.

Both words, anglicized, made their initial appearance in England soon afterwards, but with reversed connotations, antisemitism becoming a negative, critical word, and philosemitism a positive, commendable one. But while antisemitism (and its variants, antisemite and antisemitic) immediately entered the English vocabulary, philosemitism was much slower in doing so; indeed it still lags far behind.[9] The *Encyclopaedia Britannica*, even in its latest (2011) edition, has a substantial entry for antisemitism, but none for philosemitism. More surprising is the current (2007) *Encyclopaedia Judaica*, which has a near-book-length article on antisemitism but none on philosemitism (and only three references to the word in the index). Nor is there any article on philosemitism (or even the word in the index) in the widely available and often quoted 1972 edition, where antisemitism occupies eighty amply illustrated pages. Yet the preface to that edition contains a tribute to its chief editor, Cecil Roth, the dean of English Jewish historians, who had died two years earlier, and who had referred to philosemitism often in his scholarly work.[10]

One of the difficulties with philosemitism is that the word itself is something of a misnomer. The literal meaning is "love of Jews" (by non-Jews, presumably). Yet "love," in this context, may be an overstatement, as the *Oxford English Dictionary* implicitly recognizes. Translating almost all the other compound words starting with "philo" as "love of" or "fondness of"—philotheism, for example, is "love of God"—the *OED* makes an exception of philosemitism, defining it as in "favor" or "support" of Jews. But if philosemitism generally implies something less than love, it also implies something more than "tolerance" or "toleration," ideas that, to a philosemite, may seem condescending or patronizing. One may tolerate, after all, that of which one disapproves. Goethe put it more eloquently: "Toleration should really only be a transitory attitude. It must lead to recognition. To tolerate is to insult."[11] Philosemitism goes beyond toleration to what Goethe, and more memorably Hegel, called "recognition"; a slave "recognizes" his master, is conscious of him as an independent and unique "spirit," while the master does not "recognize" the slave.* On some occasions and for some Christians—Evangelicals, most notably—philosemitism goes beyond recognition to reverence or adulation, something very like "love."

More familiar than the word "philosemitism" is an expression often associated with it, "the people of the book." This too has a curious history. It is said to have originated with Mohammed and appears for the first time, and repeatedly, in the Koran. "The people of the book" are Jews and Christians as distinct from Muslims; and the "book" is the Bible, the Old and New Testaments, as distinct from the Koran. The expression sometimes has a benign connotation: "And there are certainly, among the People of the Book those who believe in God, in the revelation to you, and in the revelation to them, bowing in humility to God."[12] But more often it has pejorative overtones, the people of that older book displaying an obstinate and ominous resistance to the newer and truer revelation.

> Ye People of the Book! Why reject ye the Signs of Allah
> of which ye are yourselves witnesses? . . . Ye People of the
> Book! Why do ye clothe truth with falsehood and conceal
> the truth while ye have knowledge? . . . If only the People
> of the Book had faith it were best for them . . . , but most of
> them are perverted transgressors.[13]

---

* It is a moot question whether this idea of recognition originated with Goethe or Hegel, who were good friends. Hegel often quoted from Goethe, his *Iphigenia* especially, and was much taken with the idea of *Sittlichkeit* (morality) expressed in that play.

Just as philosemitism was converted from a negative to a positive term, so was "the people of the book." English Protestants—Puritans, especially—proudly adopted it for themselves to describe the Bible-centered culture that distinguished them from Catholics and foreigners. It was in the early seventeenth century, according to the Victorian historian John Richard Green, that "England became the people of a book, and that book was the Bible."[14] Although the Bible included, of course, the Old and New Testaments, it was the Old Testament, the "Hebrew Bible," as Matthew Arnold said, that was "the Book of the Nations."[15] For Evangelicals, the Hebrew Bible, was identified more specifically with one nation, the Hebrew nation—"God's ancient people" (in Lord Shaftesbury's famous phrase).[16] It is in this sense that "the people of the book" is generally understood today—the Jewish people heir to that most ancient book.

Some Jewish historians, all too aware of the painful realities of antisemitism, find little evidence of philosemitism and do not credit much of what passes as such. Todd Endelman, writing about English Jewry in the eighteenth and early nineteenth centuries, describes many religious philosemites, who promoted causes favorable to Jews, as "hostile" because they looked forward to their conversion, thus seeking to destroy their very existence as Jews.[17] Anthony Julius, in his history of antisemitism in England, raises the provocative question, "Are philosemites irrational enemies of the Jews?" Many, he says, are not so much philosemites as anti-antisemites. "They write out of reason, not love; they regard the Jew 'as just like anyone else'." Others send out "mixed signals" which may confirm antisemites in their distaste for Jews. Professing to admire Jews for heroically enduring centuries of persecution, they describe, all too graphically, the stereotypically disagreeable Jewish traits resulting from that unhappy history. Still others are so ardent in their praise of Jews that "ostensible compliments" become "covert disparagements."[18]

Even today, the effusive rhetoric of some philosemites may strike an uncomfortably discordant note. One character in Disraeli's novel *Coningsby* lauds the "pure race" that dominates the intellectual, financial, and diplomatic life in Europe, ending in a roll call of ministers of finance most of whom are Jewish[19]; *The Protocols of the Elders of Zion* could not have said it better. Or there is Winston Churchill's description of Jews as "the most formidable and the most remarkable race which has ever appeared in the world"[20]—an incitement, perhaps, to the antisemite who finds that "race" all the more fearful and hateful precisely because it is so "formidable."

In these cases, it was not the word "race" itself that was pejorative or even provocative. In England, well into the nineteenth century (for some Englishmen, well into the twentieth), "race" was not an invidious term. In 1925 Lloyd George spoke of his beloved Welsh as an "ancient race," although not as ancient as the Jews.[21] Almost thirty years later, responding to the tributes paid to him on his eightieth birthday, Churchill used it proudly to refer to his beloved country. "It [England] was a nation and a race dwelling all around the globe that had the lion's heart. I had the luck to be called upon to give the roar."[22] What might be deemed offensive was not the idea of the Jews as a race but the extravagant praise heaped upon them, confirming the worst suspicions and resentments of those implicitly assigned to an inferior race.

Philosemitism, in its many forms and degrees, has its own ambiguities. It also has a rich history in English society, politics, diplomacy, and literature. If the excessive rhetoric of some philosemites sends out "mixed signals," the modest rhetoric of others may send out no signals at all, yet still be an important presence in political and social life as well as in public discourse. Philosemitism, it may be argued, has been so much a part of modern England that it is not always recognized or labelled as such. Just as antisemitism may be casual or covert—"social antisemitism," or "country-club" antisemitism as it is known in America—so there is a familiar form of "social philosemitism," the respectful attitude that most Englishmen, in most circumstances, have extended to Jews. Nor is toleration as demeaning as Goethe thought. Someone moved by the spirit of toleration, writing "out of reason, not love," and regarding the Jew as "just like anyone else" (or like oneself), is according him a considerable measure of "recognition"—of respect, if not love. This is no mean virtue, certainly by contrast to the antisemite who does not write out of reason, let alone love; who does not regard the Jew like anyone else, let alone like oneself; and who is not inclined to tolerate Jews in any sphere of life. Moreover, toleration coexists comfortably with philosemitism; indeed it may even inspire sentiments that resemble philosemitism.

A proper history of English philosemitism would take all the species of philosemitism, in all their manifestations and complexities, into account, placing them within a comprehensive narrative of modern Anglo-Jewish history. This book is not that history. It is rather a historical essay highlighting crucial ideas and events in that history, from the readmission of the Jews to England in the seventeenth century, through the discourses and disputes of the eighteenth, culminating in the admission to full citizenship in the nineteenth, and beyond that to the achievement of Jewish statehood in the twentieth. To convey the spirit as well as the substance of that history, I have quoted extensively from contemporary speeches and writings, especially by those eminent Englishmen who have, in other memorable ways, shaped the history of their country. Summaries and paraphrases cannot do justice to the varieties and subtleties of philosemitism exhibited on these occasions, or to the passion that inspired them and their audiences. Ideally, this essay should be accompanied by the full texts of these documents. Short of that, lengthy quotations, placed in context, may serve to illuminate the past, inform the present, and, perhaps, inspire the future, recalling England to its "past glory."

I.

In the Beginning:
The Readmission of the Jews

There is a poetic justice—or historic justice—in England's relation to Jews. A notable exemplar of philosemitism in modern times, England was also a notable exemplar of anti-semitism in medieval times. It has two dubious "firsts" to its credit: it was the first country, in 1144, to instigate a "blood libel" case (the charge that the blood of Christian children was used in Jewish religious rituals), and the first country, in 1290, to expel the Jews, an expulsion that was more complete than the more notorious one two centuries later in Spain.

Winston Churchill, in his *History of the English-Speaking Peoples*, has a graphic account of that event:

> Edward saw himself able to conciliate powerful elements and
> escape from awkward debts, by the simple and well-trodden
> path of anti-Semitism. The propaganda of ritual murder and
> other dark tales, the commonplaces of our enlightened age,
> were at once invoked with general acclaim. The Jews, held
> up to universal hatred, were pillaged, maltreated, and finally
> expelled [from] the realm. Exception was made for certain

physicians without whose skill persons of consequence might have lacked due attention. Once again the sorrowful, wandering race, stripped to the skin, must seek asylum and begin afresh. To Spain or North Africa the melancholy caravan, now so familiar, must move on. Not until four centuries had elapsed was Oliver Cromwell by furtive contracts with a moneyed Israelite to open again the coasts of England to the enterprise of the Jewish race. It was left to a Calvinist dictator to remove the ban which a Catholic king had imposed.[1]

With his unerring instinct for the drama of history, Churchill went to the heart of the matter: after almost four centuries, a Calvinist removed the ban imposed by a Catholic. It is interesting to find him defining that event not in terms of Christian and Jew, but of Calvinist and Catholic, reminding us of the role Protestantism played in Jewish history. It was a Protestant ruler who brought the Jews back to England. By the same token, we may be reminded of the role Judaism played in English history. It was to the Hebrew Bible that Henry VIII looked for the legitimization of his divorce from Catherine of Aragon, which was the initial impetus for the English Reformation. Because the Biblical sources were conflicting (Catherine was his dead brother's widow, a marriage specifically proscribed in Leviticus and just as specifically prescribed in Deuteronomy), Christian Hebraic scholars were imported from the continent to resolve this problem, inspiring English scholars to engage in the serious study of the Hebrew language and Hebrew texts. In 1536, Henry established Regius Professorships of Hebrew at Oxford and Cambridge, a formal initiation, so speak, of the Hebraist movement which produced the "authorized" King James version of the Bible in 1611. From the perspective of his own day, a Victorian historian was especially appreciative of the profound moral change that that translation brought to the culture of England.

> England became the people of a book, and that book was the Bible. It was as yet the one English book which was familiar to every Englishman: it was read in churches and read at home and everywhere its words, as they fell on ears which custom had not yet deadened, kindled a startling enthusiasm. What the revival of classical learning had done on the Continent was done in England in a far profounder fashion by the translation of the Scriptures.[2]

It was not only the popular culture that was so profoundly changed. Hebraism permeated the high culture as well, for it involved considerably more than the familiar Bible-reading and Bible-quoting in English. It required a scholarly knowledge of Hebrew, and not only of the Old Testament but also of the more esoteric Hebrew texts—the Talmud, Maimonides, and even the Kabbalah. Moreover it was not only Hebraic scholars who read and studied these writings. They were known, to one degree or another, by people of all callings—preachers, pamphleteers, poets, politicians, philosophers; and by people of all ideological dispositions—republican, monarchical, religious, even secular. Of the 150 sermons delivered in the Long Parliament between 1640 and 1645, five times as many were devoted to the Old Testament as to the New—and this by Presbyterians and Anglicans as well as Puritans.[3]

Even Hobbes, reputed to be the most materialistic and atheistic of philosophers, qualifies as a Hebraist. Much of the second half of the *Leviathan* is devoted to quotations from the Scriptures, mainly from the Old Testament, designed to demonstrate that the covenant creating society originated with the covenant of God with Abraham and carried out by "Moses the Sovereign Prophet." "In short," Hobbes concluded, "the Kingdom of God is a Civil Kingdom, which consisted first in the obligation of the people of Israel to those laws which Moses should bring unto them from Mount Sinai," later to be delivered by the High Priest, and only finally to be "restored by Christ."[4] Hobbes may have meant this theological exegesis as window-dressing for his heretical (in Cromwellian England) political views. But it is significant that he felt the need to invoke Scripture at such length, that he was knowledgeable enough to do so, and that his readers were comfortable with his endless Biblical quotations and allusions.[*]

The Hebraicization, so to speak, of the culture occurred before there were any Jews in England, or at least any Jews publicly known to be such. But it did focus attention upon the Jews, the primordial "people of the book"—the Hebrew book. As early as 1621 one venturesome Hebraist scoured the Bible for predictions about the return of the Jews to their ancient land. Sir Henry Finch, a distinguished lawyer and legal scholar, published his findings, anonymously, in a book with a formidable title: *The World's Resurrection or The Calling of the Jews. A Present to Judah and the Children of Israel that Joined with Him, and to Joseph (that Valiant Tribe of Ephraim) and all the House of Israel that Joined with Him.* The dedication, in Hebrew, repeating part of the title, adds: "The Lord give them [the Jews] grace, that they may return and seek Jehovah their God, and David their King, in these latter days." Moreover, it was not individual Jews who were to return but the entire people: "Out of all the places of thy dispersion, East, West, North,

---

[*] *Leviathan* was published in 1651, at the very time the readmission of the Jews began to be discussed. Although Hobbes returned to England shortly afterwards (he had been living in France), he played no part in the subsequent debate.

and South, his purpose is to bring thee home again, and to marry thee to himself by faith for evermore." In precise, almost legalistic terms, Finch analyzed the Biblical evidence for that return, insisting that the terms he used—"Israel, Judah, Zion, Jerusalem"—were meant not spiritually or allegorically but literally and specifically. "Israel" referred not to "the church of God" in the general sense which might include "Jews and Gentiles," but to "Jews" alone—"Israel properly descended out of Jacob's loins." And their return was not only to their ancient land but to a "body politic," a "kingdom of Jerusalem" which would be recognized by all other kingdoms, including those of the Gentiles.[5]

It was in the reign of James I that Finch issued this bold manifesto, which was far too Puritanical in spirit for the liking of a firmly Episcopalian monarch, and was especially offensive because it suggested that the English king would have to recognize as his equal a king of the Jews. Finch, who had dedicated one of his earlier books to James and whose legal disquisitions had been agreeable to him, was now *persona non grata*. He and his publisher were arrested, their houses and possessions confiscated, and their licenses revoked. Finch was released from jail only after recanting his "ill-advised" book. He died shortly afterwards—ironically, in the same year as James.

Toward the middle of the century, when the monarchy itself was in peril, Hebraism was fortified by another spiritual movement that had momentous consequences for the absent Jews. Like many Hebraists, Finch envisaged the ultimate conversion of the Jews, but this was not his immediate interest. It was, however, for Millenarians, who sought the conversion of Jews as the precondition for the Second Coming of Christ. And because that conversion, it was widely believed, could take place only in England where the Gospel could be taught in its purest form, the return of the Jews to England took priority over their return to Israel. Thus Millenarianism, flourishing in this period of religious and political upheaval, provided a powerful impulse for the readmission of the Jews to England after centuries of exile.

Among the other revolutionary ideas that emerged in this tumultuous time that which had an obvious bearing upon the Jews was the doctrine of toleration. Initially extended to Baptists and some other Protestant sects, it could be applied to Jews as well. Indeed, it might be applied to Jews more easily than to Catholics (or even Episcopalians), who were still regarded as the enemies of the Commonwealth. Although that doctrine was purely secular and political in principle, it was imbued with religious sentiments which were pervasive and compelling. "The Arraignment of Mr. Persecution," a pamphlet in 1645 by the Leveller leader Richard Overton, argued for the toleration of all faiths, but even there the Biblical overtones were evident, for among those who were to be tolerated were the Jews, "the apple of God's eye."[6] In the famous tract, "The Bloudy Tenent of Persecution," by the American Roger Williams, religion figured not merely rhetorically but substantively.* Published in London in 1644 while he was on a visit there (and publicly burned, by order of Parliament, while he was returning to America), the book is as much a work of Biblical exegesis as it is of public policy. Indeed, much of the argument for toleration is based on Scripture—the Old Testament prefiguring the New (but also sometimes in conflict with it) and the New consummating the Old. "It is the will and command of God," Williams declared as one of his opening principles,

---

* *The Bloudy Tenent* is commonly referred to as a "tract," but the word does not quite do justice to the five-hundred-page book, including the reply by his arch-critic John Cotton and Williams's counter-reply, both of which are densely theological. That it should have had the audience and influence it did is itself, quite apart from its message, a tribute to the prevailing Hebraist culture, in America as well as England.

that "the coming of his Son the Lord Jesus, a permission of the most Paganish, Jewish, Turkish or antichristian consciences and worships be granted to all men in all nations and countries; and they are only to be fought against with that sword which is only, in soul matters, able to conquer: to wit, the sword of God's Spirit, the word of God."[7]

In a sequel to the book, replying to the objection that toleration would undermine society as well as religion, Williams put the case for toleration in terms that would appeal to the secular-minded as well as the religious: "A false religion and worship will not hurt the civil state, in case the worshippers broke no civil law; . . . and the civil laws not being broken, civil peace is not broken; and this only is the point in question."[8] On a second visit to England in 1652, Williams addressed the question raised by a parliamentary committee: whether it was the duty of the magistrate "to permit the Jews, whose conversion we look for, to live freely and peaceably among us?" Williams's answer was unequivocal: "I humbly conceive it to be the duty of the civil magistrate to break down that superstitious wall of separation (as to civil things) between us Gentiles and the Jews, and freely (without their asking) to make way for their free and peaceable habitation amongst us."[9] (This was the first usage of the expression "wall of separation" that was to figure so momentously in the history of the United States.)

Another pamphlet was still more effusive in support of the Jews, and particularly in favor of their readmission to England. "An Apology for the Honorable Nation of the Jews, and all the sons of Israel," published in 1649 by an "Edward Nicholas, Gent," reasoned that England's present troubles were the result of "the strict and cruel laws now in force against the most honorable nation of the world, the nation of the Jews, a people chosen by God." Unless the English atoned by readmitting the Jews, "God will charge their sufferings upon us, and will avenge them on their persecutors." He himself, the author assured his readers, was motivated by "the glory of God, the comfort of those his afflicted people, the love of my own sweet native country of England, and the freeing of my own soul in the day of account."[10]

It is against this background of Hebraism, millenarianism, and toleration—characterized by such notable historians as Cecil Roth and David Katz as "philosemitic"—that Cromwell was called on to consider the readmission of the Jews after the centuries of their exile.[11] The "Calvinist dictator" described by Churchill (a "reluctant and apologetic" dictator) also saw good economic and political reasons for their readmission.[12] By the mid-seventeenth century, the "New Christians"—Marranos, converted crypto-Jews who had filtered back to England from Spain and Portugal—had already proved to be a valuable financial asset to the government and to the country. And they could be even more valuable if Jews from the continent, and from Holland in particular, were encouraged to come to England, bringing with them the economic talents that had contributed to the prosperity of England's chief commercial rival and military enemy.

The subject of the readmission of the Jews took a practical, political turn in December 1648, when a new constitution for England, the Instrument of Government, was being considered. One resolution called for the toleration for all religions, "not excepting Turks, nor Papists, nor Jews"; another recommended the repeal of the act banishing Jews. In January the Council of Officers received a petition written by two English Puritans living in Amsterdam, Joanna Cartwright and her son Ebenezer, proposing that "this nation of England, with the inhabitants of the Netherlands, shall be the first and the readiest to transport Israel's sons and daughters in their ships to the land promised to their forefathers, Abraham, Isaac and Jacob for an everlasting inheritance." For this purpose, it was necessary that the Jews "may again be received and permitted to trade and dwell amongst you in this land." The Council did not reject this petition but nullified it, in effect, by decreeing that religious freedom be reserved to those who "profess faith in God by Jesus Christ."[13]

Another petition, again from Amsterdam, carried more weight and was discussed more seriously. This came from the leading Dutch rabbi, Menasseh ben Israel (who may have inspired the Cartwrights). A scholar, mystic, and Jewish millenarian, he had been much impressed by a Marrano returning from Ecuador who reported on a group of natives who spoke Hebrew, practiced Jewish rituals, and were believed to be of the lost tribes of Reuben and Levi. If the dispersion had spread to that remote part of the world, the rabbi reasoned, England remained the only country where there were no Jews (at least none recognized as such). And since their total dispersion was the precondition for the Jewish messianic deliverance, their return to England was crucial. This was the message of Menasseh ben Israel's book *The Hope of Israel*. Written in Latin and immediately translated and published in England in 1650 (with a dedication to the English Parliament), it was an instant success, going through three editions in as many years. It appealed especially to the Hebraists who were much taken with the citations from Deuteronomy, the Book of Daniel, and medieval texts, which seemed to confirm the account of dispersion and redemption.*

The author hoped to deliver his message in person, but because of the war between the two countries, it was not until

---

* The medieval commentators, mistaking the etymology of the French word *Angleterre*, "Land of the Angles," translated it as *ketzei ha-aretz*, the "extremity of the earth," suggesting that England was the final place of dispersion that would lead to the millennium.[14]

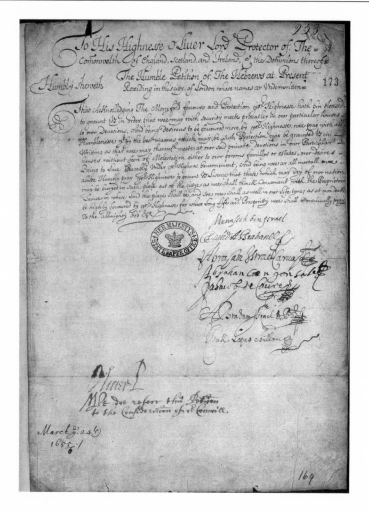

FIGURE 1 Petition to Cromwell by Menasseh ben Israel, 1656, National
Archives SP 18/125, f.173. Copyright © National Archives

1655 that he was able to come to England, bringing with him "The Humble Addresses of Menasseh ben Israel, a Divine and Doctor of Physick, in behalf of the Jewish Nation." (The original text was in French.) This not so humble petition called upon "His Highness the Lord Protector of the Commonwealth of England, Scotland, and Ireland" to readmit the Jews under specified conditions: the free exercise of religion, the right to establish and maintain synagogues and cemeteries, the repeal of all laws against the Jews, an oath by public officials to defend Jews, the right of Jews to try cases by Mosaic law subject to appeal by civil judges, and the unrestricted right of Jews to trade. The Jewish immigrants, in return, would swear allegiance to the English government and would be kept under strict surveillance.

Menasseh ben Israel had good reason to think that the Lord Protector would be well disposed to his appeal. Two years earlier, toward the end of his opening address to Parliament, Cromwell quoted the sixty-eighth Psalm and called upon the English to fulfill its "glorious prophecy."

> Truly seeing things are thus, that you are at the edge of
> the Promises and Prophecies. . . . There [the 68th Psalm] it
> prophesies that "He will bring His People again from the
> depth of the sea," as He once led Israel through the Red Sea.
> And it may be, as some think, God will bring the Jews home
> to their station, "from the isles of the sea" and answer their
> expectations "as from the depths of the sea". . . . It shall be
> a gathering of people as "out of deep waters," "out of the
> multitude of waters": such are His People, drawn out of
> the multitudes of the nations and peoples of this world. . . .
> And indeed the triumph of that Psalm is exceeding high and
> great, and God is accomplishing it.[15]

Submitted to Cromwell on October 31, 1655, the petition was turned over for consideration to a committee of the Council of State. Two weeks later the Council reported the committee's recommendation: "that, the Jews deserving it, may be admitted into this nation to trade and traffic and dwell amongst us as providence shall give occasion."[16] Questions raised by some members on the advisability of unlimited immigration were referred to yet another body, the Whitehall Conference. Presided over by Cromwell himself on December 4, the Conference heard the reading of the petition and then adjourned, to reconvene three days later for the debate. That debate and others in later sessions were serious and civil. One of the participants, commenting on the "very great injuries, and cruelties, and murders" inflicted on the Jews, found this was all the more deplorable because even after the Jews had rejected Christ, they still remained his chosen people, "beloved for their Fathers sakes."[17] The two jurists in the Conference pointed out that there was, in fact, no law forbidding the return of the Jews; the 1290 edict expelling them had been based on a royal prerogative and applied only to the individuals concerned. This seemed so compelling an argument that John Evelyn prematurely reported in his diary, "Now were the Jews admitted."[18] Opponents of the petition, however, raised economic as well as religious objections. Merchants feared the competition of the newcomers, and clerics were prepared to accept only those adhering to the faith of Jesus.

The most extensive and forceful argument against the petition came not from the Conference or the Council but from an outsider, the polemicist and pamphleteer William Prynne. Once an ardent Puritan, he had became an equally ardent Erastian, favoring a strict control of the state over all religious matters. His pamphlet, *A Short Demurrer to the Jews' Long Discon-*

tinued Remitter into England, was a chronicle of records and documents bearing upon the Jews going back to medieval times, intended to give a scholarly basis for the argument against their readmission. The documents themselves have earned the plaudits of later historians, including Jews, who have praised the work as "a monument of learning as well as of acerbity," and have hailed Prynne as "the father of medieval Anglo-Jewish historiography."[19] Interspersed with the documents, however, are more than acerbic comments about the people who are the subject of that chronicle.

> A most rebellious, disobedient, gainsaying, stiff-necked, impenitent, incorrigible, adulterous, whorish, impudent, froward, shameless, perverse, treacherous, revolting, backsliding, idolatrous, wicked, sinful, stubborn, untoward, hard-hearted, hypocritical people . . . given up to a blind, obdurate, obstinate, impenitent, stupid heart and spirit, a reprobate sense, a cauterized conscience. . . . How can or dare we then receive into our Christian island, such barbarous, bloody, obstinate murderers . . . ?[20]

Widely distributed among the public as well as in government circles, the *Demurrer* may well have tilted the balance against the petition.

On the 18th of December, when it was evident that the Conference could not come to a decision, Cromwell entered the chamber and berated the participants. To those objecting to the admission of non-Christians, he pointed out that it was precisely the Christian's duty to admit the Jews to England, the only country where they could be taught religion in its purity, and "not to exclude them from the light and leave them among false teachers, Papists and idolators." He rebuked the City men representing the interests of merchants who had so little faith in themselves. "Can you really be afraid that this mean and despised people should be able to prevail in trade over the merchants of England, the noblest and most esteemed merchants of the whole world?" The readmission of the Jews, he assured them, was in accord with Scripture, and so long as there was promise of their conversion, they should be "permitted to reside where the Gospel was preached." A commentator on that session reported: "His Highness was eager for the scheme, if so it might be." But it was not to be. When the Conference could not come to a conclusion, Cromwell dismissed it, taking it upon himself and the Council to resolve the problem for the glory of God and the good of the nation.[21]

The issue was not, in fact, resolved by Cromwell and the Council. It was settled the following year by the courts as the result of a simple judicial decision. With the outbreak of war with Spain the preceding autumn, the property of Spanish Marranos living in England had been expropriated. One of them, a wealthy merchant named Antonio Robles, submitted a petition for the restitution of his property on the grounds that he was not a Spaniard but a Portuguese "of the Hebrew nation." On May 16, 1656 the Council judged in his favor and ordered his property returned. "As a Spanish Catholic," Cecil Roth comments, "his position had been open to question. As a refugee Jew he was safe."[22] Thus the readmission of Jews to England was achieved by simply affirming the status quo, recognizing Jews as legal residents of England.

This judicial—not parliamentary—decision confirmed what Cromwell was doing in practice. Even while the Council was still debating the issue, a contemporary report described him as "conniving" to allow Jews greater latitude in religious matters, recognizing their right, for example, to worship privately in their homes.[23] After the Robles decision, that latitude was extended. Permission was granted for the lease of a house as a synagogue and for the establishment of a cemetery. A Jew was admitted to the Stock Exchange as a broker without having to take the Christian oath. And Cromwell personally authorized the grant to Menasseh ben Israel of an annual state pension of a hundred pounds a year. (He did not have long to enjoy the pension. He died in 1657.)

Scholars have been wary of interpreting this event, and particularly Cromwell's role in it, in the familiar "Whig history" mode, seeing history as the ineluctable progress toward a more liberal, enlightened, tolerant—and secular—age.[24] In 1828, William Godwin (a radical rather than a Whig) provided just such an interpretation in his *History of the Commonwealth*. He then paid tribute to Cromwell (whom he disagreed with in other respects) as "sincere in his religion, fervent in his patriotism, and earnestly devoted to the best interest of mankind." He particularly admired Cromwell's "resolve" to readmit the Jews on the principle of toleration rather than religion.

> It was an enterprise worthy of his character. His comprehensive mind enabled him to take in all its recommendations and all its advantages. The liberality of his disposition, and his avowed attachment to the cause of toleration, rendered it an adventure becoming him to achieve. As a man, he held that no human being should be proscribed among his fellowmen for the accident of his birth.[25]

This was not quite the Cromwell contemporaries knew. Churchill's Cromwell was closer to the truth. It was as a Calvinist dictator, if a reluctant one, in a thoroughly religious spirit as well as a practical one, that Cromwell favored the readmission of the

Jews. And the debate at the time reflected the religious passions of the protagonists as well as their economic interests.

If the "Whig fallacy" warns us against an overly secular view of the progress of history, it also warns us against too benign a view of those who professed to be progressive—enlightened, rational, tolerant. Even some of those who vigorously supported the principle of toleration and are generally identified with that cause revealed an antipathy to Jews that often overrode that principle. Seeking toleration for themselves, some Dissenters vigorously opposed extending that toleration to others. The Quakers who are now the most tolerant and unbigoted of sects, were, in this early period of their history under the leadership of their founder, George Fox, notably intolerant of others, including, or especially, Jews. In 1656, at the very time that the readmission of the Jews was still in question, Fox petitioned Cromwell to alleviate the situation of Quakers, who were being harassed for their aggressively anti-clerical, anti-political, and, often, anti-social behavior. Yet Fox himself was zealously anti-Jewish, denouncing Judaism as a corrupt, legalistic, pharisaic religion and inveighing against Jews as "Christ killers," the "persecutors of Christ."[26]

Hebraism itself might have equivocal effects. The most renowned of the Hebraists was the leading jurist of the time and Member of Parliament John Selden, whose biographer has bestowed upon him the honorary title of "Renaissance England's Chief Rabbi."[27] His book *On Natural Law* (written in Latin, as all his works were) focused on the Noahide laws, the seven commandments of the sons of Noah that were incumbent upon non-Jews as much as on Jews. In effect, Selden legitimized natural law by deriving it from Jewish law. Another of his books, on Jewish marital and divorce laws, was intended as a model for the reform of English laws. More ambitious was his three-volume work on the Sanhedrin, the judicial court of ancient Israel. Published in 1650–1655 (at a time when the English constitution was under consideration), it suggested a close parallel between the Sanhedrin and the English Parliament. Each of these works (citing Maimonides and other Hebrew scholars) was directed against those Protestants—Presbyterians, for the most part— who regarded Jewish traditions and precedents not as models to be emulated but as evils to be refuted and eliminated. Selden himself, however, knew few living Jews and had little concern for their conditions or status. Indeed, some occasional passing references to them were belittling or derogatory. Yet the undeniable effect of his work was to elevate Hebrew texts, laws, and institutions, giving them an authority and practical relevance for England at a critical time of its history.

A great admirer of Selden was James Harrington, whose work, although less scholarly than Selden's, was perhaps more influential, if only because he wrote in English rather than Latin, and because his major book was in the guise of a utopia. (His utopia was also more influential than the earlier utopia, *New Atlantis*, by the more eminent philosopher, Francis Bacon.)* Published in 1656 and dedicated to Cromwell, Harrington's *Commonwealth of Oceana* was a thinly disguised prospectus for the Commonwealth of England, spelling out in detail the constitution for a reformed England that would be republican, egalitarian, and predominantly agrarian. The Commonwealth of Oceana, Harrington explained, was inspired by the republics

---

* Bacon's utopia, *New Atlantis*, published posthumously in 1627, features one Jew (a "circumcized" Jew, it is specified) who instructs the narrator in the laws and customs of the country regarding marriage and family (all very chaste and virtuous, unlike, Bacon observes, another Utopia—Thomas More's, obviously—where the couple are permitted to see each other naked before marriage). That Jew was "a wise man and learned, and of great policy."[28] Later scholars have identified his prototype as a Bohemian (Czech) engineer, Joachim Gaunse, then living in England, who in 1584 was sent by Sir Walter Raleigh to America to develop its mining resources, and who thus became the first Jew to set foot on English soil in North America.[29]

of Rome and Venice but principally by the "Commonwealth of Israel." Unlike Hobbes who invoked the Old Testament as the ideal monarchy, Harrington cited it as the ideal republic, describing, admiringly and at length, the institutions of ancient Israel (including the division of powers and rulers chosen by the people), which were a model for Oceana and thus for England.[30]*

Modern Jews make their appearance toward the end of *Oceana*, perhaps as an afterthought prompted by the readmission debate. (Although published in 1656, most of the book had been written earlier.) On the penultimate page of this two-hundred-odd-page book, Harrington created a mini-utopia, so to speak, for Jews—not in Oceana itself but in the neighboring island of Panopea (i.e., Ireland). Panopea, "the soft mother of a slothful and pusillanimous people," had been depopulated and repopulated with a new race, the Anglo-Irish, but they too had degenerated. Yet the island's soil was rich and its ports commodious, and if it had been resettled with Jews, "allowing them their own rites and laws," they would have come in great numbers from all over the world. Moreover, they would have come as farmers as well as merchants (as they had been in Canaan before their exile), thereby contributing to the desirable agrarian nature of the economy. Had that happened, all would have been well in that unfortunate island: "Panopea, being farmed out to the Jews and their heirs forever . . . [under specified expenditures of money and income] . . . , would have been a bargain of

---

* Although generically the word "commonwealth" simply meant government, in this context it was equated with "republic," partly because of its association with the Cromwellian Commonwealth. It is interesting how often, in the Anglo-Hebraist literature, ancient Israel is referred to as a "republic"—*respublica Hebraeorum*. What was technically a monarchy was deemed to be a republic in spirit, based upon the books of Judges and Samuel which were anti-monarchic, and a kingship that was not hereditary and was subject both to the will of God and, as God told Samuel, the "voice of the people."

such advantage, both to them and this commonwealth, as is not to be found otherwise by either."

Only at the very end of this mini-Jewish-utopia in Panopea does it appear that it is not quite so utopian. "To receive the Jews," the concluding sentence reads, "after any other manner into a commonwealth were to maim it; for they of all nations never incorporate, but taking up the room of a limb, are no use to the body, while they suck the nourishment which would sustain a natural and useful member."[31] Oceana itself may appear to be something less than utopian, for that commonwealth, ostensibly modeled on the Hebraic republic, is utopian only because it is unencumbered by Jews—that useless "limb" sucking out the nourishment from an otherwise healthy body.

It was later said, by cynical critics, that Christian Zionists sought a homeland for the Jews in Israel so as to remove them from the countries they currently inhabited. This, in effect, was exactly what Harrington was proposing for Oceana. At just the time when the readmission of the Jews to England was being considered, he suggested admitting them not to Oceana, his utopian England, but only to the neighboring "degenerate" island of Panopea, where they could serve a useful purpose. The only reference to Jews in Oceana itself is a negative one. Earlier in the book, the principle of "liberty of conscience" is applied to those whose worship was "not Popish, Jewish, nor Idolatrous."[32]

That Hebraism did not always signify a favorable disposition towards Jews is demonstrated by another much acclaimed Hebraist, John Milton. Puritan, republican, revolutionary, the scourge of King and Church, Milton is the hero of latter-day radicals, liberals, and civil libertarians. *Areopagitica*, published in 1644 during the Civil War, is still hailed as the classic declaration of the freedom of speech and press (with the caveat, to be sure, that that freedom did not apply to "popery and open superstition," or that which is "impious" and "against faith or manners").[33] A serious Hebraist, Milton read the Bible in Hebrew, studied commentaries on the Scriptures as well as Maimonides and other Medieval sages, wrote learned theological discourses and Biblical exegeses—and, most memorably, left us a body of poetry steeped in the themes, imagery, and language of the Old Testament.

Yet even Milton's admirers have cause for doubt and dismay. A careful reading of both his poetry and prose reveals inconsistencies and ambiguities in his renditions of the Old Testament and, more disturbing, a profound ambivalence toward Judaism itself. The title of an essay on Milton perfectly expresses this ambivalence: "Milton's Dichotomy of 'Judaism' and 'Hebraism'."[34] Hebraism represented the positive, pro-Jewish side of Milton, Judaism the negative, anti-Jewish side. These were not inconsistencies or ambiguities on Milton's part, this scholar maintains, but rather a conscious, sustained duality in his thinking, evident in his poetry but especially in his prose. Moreover, the dichotomy is not the familiar one between the ancient and moderns, between the ideal Jews of the Old Testament and the all too real and fallible Jews today. It is more fundamental and profound, appearing within Scripture itself. The Hebraic element is the "spirit" of the Old Testament, the universal, moral principle represented by the covenant of the Jews with God; it is this spirit that is a model for the English people. The Judaic element, however, is the dead "letter" of the Old Testament, the entire body of Mosaic law, including the rites and rituals prescribed in the Bible as well as the positive laws laid down by Moses and the rabbis. All of these Milton contemned as superstitious and pharisaic, a "curse" and a "death." (The only exception was the law on divorce, of which he approved, at a time when his own marriage was troubled and he was contemplating divorce). And the historic people of the Bible, so far from being a model for the English, he vilified as "servile" Israelites, in "bondage" to the law, little more than "Judaizing beasts."[35]

Unlike most Hebraists who celebrated the "Hebraic republic," Milton saw in the Bible only a despicable and dangerous Jewish monarchy. In the early 1640s, he urged the Church of England to purge itself of its Judaic ceremonies and laws, reminding them that the Gospels had abrogated just those ceremonies and laws. And in the 1660s, he warned the English not to do as the Jews had done: "to put our necks again under kingship, as was made use of by the Jews to return back to Egypt and to the worship of their idol queen."[36] Whatever millenarian and conversion sentiments he expressed on other occasions, they were in abeyance as he contemplated the dispersion of the Jews, which he saw as a punishment—in perpetuity—for their iniquities, a lesson to others as well as to themselves.

> [The existence of God] is proved also by the dispersion of the ancient nation of the Jews throughout the whole world, conformably to what God often forewarned them would happen on account of their sins. Nor is it only to pay the penalty of their own guilt that they have been reserved in their scattered state, among the rest of the nations, through the revolution of successive ages, and even to the present day; but also to be a perpetual and living testimony to all people under heaven, of the existence of God, and of the truth of the Holy Scriptures.[37]*

---

* One of the sins responsible for their dispersion, Milton noted, was usury: "Their hearts were set upon usury, and are to this day, no nation more [so]." Quoting this, and observing that money-lending had been his father's occupation and a major source of Milton's own income, one scholar wonders Milton's reluctance to admit Jews to England was because they might be competitors for his trade.[38]

One scholar, concluding her account of the "fierceness" of Milton's "theological anti-Judaic attitude" (comparable, she said, to that of Prynne), wryly observed: "We would *like* Milton, the most deeply Hebraic of English literary writers, to have supported the readmission of the Jews and their toleration. That would fit our cherished notion of the liberal Milton."[39] If Milton did not, like Prynne, publicly come out against their readmission, it was probably because, as an official in Cromwell's government, it would have been impolitic to speak out against a policy that Cromwell strongly favored. But there is no doubt that the liberal Milton, the champion of freedom of speech and press, displayed toward living Jews the same "anti-Judaic attitude" that appeared in his theological writings. Yet it is *Paradise Lost* that is Milton's great legacy, and it is this epic that brought the Hebrew Bible into the permanent canon not only of English literature but of world literature.[*]

The story of the readmission of the Jews to England is full of such anomalies and ambivalences. In this respect, as in others, it anticipated the future course of Anglo-Jewish history. The readmission came through the back-door, so to speak—not because of the petition by Menasseh ben Israel, or the efforts of Cromwell and parliamentarians, nor even because of the teachings of Hebraists and the aspirations of millenarians (although these always lurked in the background), but as the result of a single law case brought by a Marrano merchant born in Portugal. Having taken refuge in England, Antonio Robles sought noth-

---

[*] John Dryden, the first official Poet Laureate (a title he acquired in 1668), pronounced *Paradise Lost*, which had been published the previous year, "one of the greatest, most noble, and most sublime poems which either this age or nation has produced."[40] If Milton was deprived of the title of laureate, it was because, with the restoration of the monarchy, he was politically as well as theologically heretical.

ing more than the return of his property, and he was granted it simply as a Jewish resident in England.

It was in this fashion, indirectly, often informally, always incrementally, that, in the course of the following centuries, English Jews attained the status they did, first as residents and then as citizens. It was also in this ambiguous manner that Hebraism and millenarianism, philosemitism and anti-Judaism played themselves out in public discourse and public policy, culminating in the acceptance of Jews as fully accredited Englishmen—and as fully accredited Jews.

II.

The Case for Toleration

It was with understandable trepidation that English Jews received the news of Cromwell's death in 1658 and the restoration of the monarchy two years later. Yet Charles II proved to be surprisingly well disposed to the Jews, reaffirming (in the face of some anti-Jewish agitation) the Crown's duty to protect them and their freedom of worship. In 1664, the Privy Council went one step further in establishing the legal residency of Jews. Responding to a petition by Jews, the Council assured them that they would enjoy "the same favor as formerly they have had, so long as they demean themselves peaceably and quietly with due obedience to his Majesty's laws and without scandal to his government."[1]

If Cromwell favored the Jews for religious as well as economic reasons, Charles, having little interest in religion, Christian or Jewish, simply found them an economic asset. James II continued that benign attitude, not out of any concern for Jews or the economy but rather in accord with the latitudinarian policy that was in the interests of Catholics. Shortly after his accession to the throne, confronted with a proposal that would have

penalized Jews for not attending church, James issued an Order
in Council reasserting the right of Jews to "quietly enjoy the free
exercise of their religion, whilst they behave themselves duti-
fully and obediently to his government."[2] The Jewish community—or communities, the Ashkenazi and Sephardi often going
their separate ways, a total of six hundred or so individuals
at the time of the Restoration—grew and prospered, and even
enjoyed, in some circles, a kind of exotic appeal. The synagogue
in London became so much a tourist attraction—Pepys visited
it at least twice, in 1662 and 1663—that the congregation had
to limit visitors in order to maintain the decorum of the service.*

The "Glorious Revolution" of 1688—a title assigned to it at
the time—may be seen as even more glorious in retrospect, for
it ushered in a century of remarkable tranquility and stability,
certainly compared with the turbulent times that preceded it. It
brought to England a monarch who was even better disposed
to Jews than his predecessors, perhaps because Dutch Jews had
helped finance William's campaign. It also brought back to England her preeminent philosopher, whose writings were to have
a pacifying effect upon the country as a whole and an especially
salutary one upon the Jewish community.

John Locke had taken refuge in Amsterdam in 1683 after
his suspected involvement in a plot to assassinate the Stuart
kings. It is fitting that the man who is often characterized as
the philosophical apologist for the Glorious Revolution should
have returned to England on February 11, 1689, in the com-

---

* Pepys's diary (October 14, 1663) describes an Orthodox service: the women behind
a "lattice out of sight," the service "all in a singing way, and in Hebrew," the "carrying
of the Torahs around the room," concluding with a prayer for the King, in Hebrew
(with his name pronounced in Portuguese). In this account, it would seem to have been
anything but decorous: "But, Lord, to see the disorder, laughing, sporting, and no attention, but confusion in all their service, more like brutes than people knowing the true
God, would make a man forswear ever seeing them more; and indeed I never did see
so much, or could have imagined there had been any religion in the whole world, so
absurdly performed as this."[3]

pany of Princess Mary of Orange, two days before the Declaration of Right deposing James and two months before the joint coronation of William and Mary. It is fitting, too, that *A Letter Concerning Toleration*, written (in Latin) while he was in exile, should have been published in English soon afterwards, translated immediately into Dutch and French, and recognized, abroad as well as in England, as the definitive statement of the principle of toleration. Roger Williams's tract earlier in the century enunciated the principle but did not give it the philosophical rigor and authority that Locke did. Nor were the official toleration acts exemplary models. The Maryland Toleration Act of 1649 provided toleration only for "trinitarian Christians," thus including Catholics but excluding Unitarians, atheists, and, of course, Jews. And the English Act of Toleration of 1689 applied only to Protestant Dissenters, granting them freedom of worship but retaining some of their disabilities, such as their exclusion from public office.

Some commentators have a restrictive interpretation of the *Letter*, reading it as denying toleration to Catholics, Muslims ("Mahometans"), and atheists. They cite Locke's assertions that Catholics and Muslims owe their allegiance to "the protection and service of another prince," and that atheists do not feel bound by the "promises, covenants, and oaths which are the bonds of human society."[4] The passage on atheists, however, qualifies that exemption: "Yet if they do not tend to establish domination over others, or civil impunity to the church in which they are taught, there can be no reason why they should not be tolerated."[5]

Indeed, the basic premise of the *Letter*, the distinction between government and religion, suggests a near-universal principle of toleration. Government has to do with life, liberty, and "things of this world," and nothing to do with "the salvation of souls" or "the world to come."[6] This distinction—the separation, in effect, of church and state—would bring within the principle of toleration not only all Protestants but all believers and non-believers, including Catholics, Muslims, pagans, atheists—and Jews.

> If a Roman Catholic believe that to be really the body of Christ, which another man calls bread, he does no injury thereby to his neighbor. If a Jew does not believe the New Testament to be the word of God, he does not thereby alter any thing in men's civil rights. If a heathen doubt of both Testaments, he is not therefore to be punished as a pernicious citizen. The power of the magistrate, and the estates of the people, may be equally secure, whether any man believe these things or no. I readily grant that these opinions are false and absurd; but the business of laws is not to provide for the truth of opinions, but for the safety and security of the commonwealth, and of every particular man's goods and person.[7]
>
>   . . . Neither pagan, nor Mahometan, nor Jew ought to be excluded from the civil rights of the commonweath, because of his religion. . . . Shall we suffer a pagan to deal and trade with us, and shall we not suffer him to pray unto and worship God? If we allow the Jews to have private houses and dwellings amongst us, why should we not allow them to have synagogues? . . . But if these things may be granted to Jews and pagans, surely the condition of any Christians ought not to be worse than theirs, in a Christian commonwealth.[8]

Whatever ambiguities one might find in other passages in the *Letter* regarding Catholics or atheists, there are none about Jews. Subject neither to a foreign power, nor wanting in morality or sense of civic duty, Jews come comfortably within the principle of toleration. They are not to be excluded because of their religion—and, by the same token, they are not to be especially favored because of it. There is nothing in the *Letter* suggestive of any religious disposition in favor of the Jews— nothing like the Leveller's description of the Jews as "the apple of God's eye," or the Puritan's identification with the Jews as "God's people," or the millenarian's reliance upon the Jews as the instrument of Christian redemption. Indeed, there are few Biblical quotations or allusions in the *Letter*. This is all the more remarkable because it is in striking contrast to Locke's *Two Treatises of Government*, written about the same time and published very soon afterwards. The *First Treatise* in particular is heavily Scriptural, in substance as well as rhetoric.[9*] Later in life, encouraged by his good friend Isaac Newton, Locke turned more seriously to Biblical studies, speculating about the conversion of Jews and their restoration to Palestine. But these reflections have no bearing upon the rest of his philosophy, let alone upon his doctrine of toleration. The *Letter* stands on its own, a bold affirmation of the principle of toleration—toleration for its own sake, not for a higher, religious end.

Unlike Locke, Newton was genuinely passionate about religion, searching the Bible for evidence of "the restoration of the Jewish nation so much spoken of by the old Prophets," as well as the Second Coming (in the year 2060, he predicted).[11] Yet he was not the mystic he is sometimes made out to be. On the contrary, he was a great admirer of Maimonides, whose rationalistic, Aristotelian mode of thought he found congenial. What Newton sought in Scripture was literal, historical evidence for the prophecies and revelations. Uncomfortable with the idea of miracles, he accepted them only for the Biblical period and the

---

* Even in respect to the *Treatises*, there is much dispute about the significance of those Biblical references, some commentators questioning whether Locke's natural law was at all dependent upon divine law.[10]

first century of Christianity, after which they were supererogatory because the divine will had no need to violate the natural order. His own credo was simple: "We must believe that there is *one God* or supreme monarch that we may fear and obey him [sic] and keep his laws and give him honor and glory. . . . We must believe that he [sic] is the God of the Jews who created the heaven and earth all things therein as is expressed in the ten commandments."[12] Most of Newton's theological exegeses were unpublished during his lifetime because they verged on heresy, and the few that did appear then or soon afterward were too erudite (and in Latin) to command public attention. Today some scholars may read them (many still in manuscript), and find in them the real, the esoteric Newton, for whom science was an appendage to religion. But the public, the historic Newton was the scientist who was known to be genuinely religious, but was revered as a scientist above all.

So, too, it was the public, the historic Locke who was esteemed as England's great philosopher and whose principle of toleration set the tone for the favorable treatment of Jews. It was in this spirit that Parliament in 1698 exempted the Jews from the onerous provisions of a bill intended to suppress blasphemy; this was the first occasion when Parliament, rather than the King and his Council, officially recognized the religious rights of Jews. The previous year a dozen Jews were admitted as brokers in the London Stock Exchange. Today that might seem a niggling concession, but at the time it was seen as a token of official as well as social acceptance. In his *History*, Winston Churchill reflected upon the spirit of the time: "The political passions of the seventeenth century had spent themselves in the closing years of Queen Anne. . . . The wrath and venom of controversy were replaced by an apathetic tolerance."[13] Churchill was not entirely happy with that turn of events; it reflected the

Whig ascendancy that kept his own party out of power for much of the century. But it was an "apathetic tolerance" much welcomed by English Jews and in striking contrast, as the historian Cecil Roth observed, to the situation of their brethren on the continent.

> Even in Holland they were excluded from certain towns and provinces, and in Turkey they received only the restricted rights of unbelievers. In Germany and Italy the ghetto system still prevailed; from Spain, Portugal, and much of France, there was complete and even barbarous exclusion; Polish Jewry was terrorized and almost rightless; Danish Jewry was insignificant. In England, on the other hand, the Jews were under the protection of the law, could settle anywhere they pleased, and enjoyed virtual social equality.[14]

That "apathetic tolerance" had its source, at least in part, in Locke's principle of toleration—a secular principle free of the ideological and religious passions, the apocalyptic visions and millenarian aspirations, which dominated the earlier period. Yet religion, in a much muted form, continued to pervade the culture and subtly modify the principle of toleration itself. Hebraism was no longer the powerful force it had been, but it was by no means dead. Perhaps the highest compliment the English could pay the Jews was to refer to their own country as "Israel" and to their own people as "Israelites." A Dissenting minister in 1719, translating the psalms, replaced the word "Israel" with "Great Britain." A sermon in 1746, during the last skirmish with the Jacobites, was dedicated to those concerned with "the welfare of our Jerusalem, and zeal for the British Israel." The title of another sermon, celebrating the victory of the English in the Seven Years War, was "The Triumph of Israelites over Moabites, or Protestants over Papists." That triumphal note was later echoed in William Blake's memorable poem "Jerusalem," which promised not to cease the good fight "Till we have built Jerusalem,/ In England's green and pleasant land."[15]

Others dealt more prosaically, but no less admiringly, with the subject of Jews. In 1712, Joseph Addison, the well-known essayist, editor of the *Spectator*, and Member of Parliament, devoted an issue of his journal to his own essay, "The Race of People Called Jews."[16] The epigram from Horace (in Latin) described the Romans growing stronger because of all the suffering they had endured. Addison applied this lesson to that other long-suffering "race," the Jews.

> As I am one, who, by my Profession, am obliged to look into all kinds of Men, there are none whom I consider with so much pleasure as those who have any thing new or extraordinary in their characters or ways of living. For this reason I have often amused myself with speculations on the race of people called *Jews*, many of whom I have met with in most of the considerable towns which I have passed through in the course of my travels. They are, indeed, so disseminated through all the trading parts of the world, that they are become the instruments by which the most distant nations converse with one another, and by which mankind are knit together in a general correspondence: They are like the pegs and nails in a great building, which, though they are but little valued in themselves, are absolutely necessary to keep the whole frame together.

Addison found the Jews remarkable, first, for their continued existence in great numbers in spite of the massacres and persecutions inflicted upon them by Christians over the ages; then, for their dispersion throughout the world, in the remotest parts of China, Africa, and America as well as Europe; and finally, for their firm adherence to their religion in spite of that baneful history. These were the "natural reasons" for their survival. The "providential reason" was the fact that they provided every age and every nation with the strongest arguments for Christianity itself. "Their number furnishes us with a sufficient cloud of witnesses that attest the truth of the Old Bible. Their dispersions spreads these witnesses through all parts of the world. The adherence to their religion makes their testimony unquestionable."[17]

This was philosemitism in its purest form—the "natural" and the "providential" in perfect accord. And this from Addison, who was not a crusading Evangelical but a mild-tempered Anglican Whig, addressing a sophisticated middle-class audience, in a popular daily whose avowed purpose was "to enliven morality with wit, and to temper wit with morality." "It was said of Socrates," Addison told his readers, "that he brought philosophy down from heaven to inhabit among men; and I shall be ambitious to have it said of me that I have brought philosophy out of closets and libraries, schools and colleges, to dwell in clubs and assemblies, at tea-tables and in coffee houses."[18] Although the *Spectator* suspended publication after two years, it continued to be read in book form throughout the eighteenth and nineteenth centuries.

The Jews found a very different champion in John Toland, an Irish polemicist, radical, and "pantheist," as he described himself—a word he coined to suggest something more heretical than deist. (Bishop Berkeley called him a "free thinker," another word of recent coinage.) Toland was also something of a Hebraist and a great admirer of Harrington, whose *Oceana* he edited. Unlike Harrington, however, who would have excluded Jews from his utopia, Toland warmly welcomed them in his Britain. In 1714, four decades before the issue of naturalization became a subject of controversy, he published *Reasons for Naturalising the Jews in Great Britain and Ireland*—naturalizing, that is, Jewish immigrants, so that they would enjoy all the privileges, and the disabilities, of English-born Jews.

An appended essay, "A Defence of the Jews against all Vulgar Prejudices in all Countries," might have been written with Harrington in mind. Ironically addressing the bishops and archbishops of Great Britain, who "as you are the advocates of the Jews at the Throne of Heaven, so you will be their friends and protectors in the British parliament," Toland recounted the history of English Jews from their "heinous" expulsion four centuries earlier and rebutted the "vulgar prejudices" against them. So far from being liabilities to England, he insisted, an increased number of Jews would be valuable assets to the country. They would not contribute to sectarian disputes, because they were indifferent to the quarrels among Protestants. They would not drain England of her wealth, because they had no other country to retire to; indeed they would bring trade and commerce to England. If they were now money-lenders, it was only because other trades had been closed to them; they had once been "shepherds in Mesopotamia, builders in Egypt, and husbandmen in their own country," and so they would now be in England. Moreover, immigration in general was desirable because a large population was conducive to productivity, prosperity, and well-being.[19]

These were good practical reasons for encouraging the immigration and naturalization of Jews. But there was something more elevating in Toland's defense of them. It is curious to find an Irish freethinker invoking the authority and echoing the arguments of the seventeenth-century Italian rabbi and scholar Simone Luzzatto, whose *Discorso circa il stato de gl'Hebrei* (*Discourse Concerning the Condition of the Jews*) had been published in Venice in 1638. It is remarkable that Toland should even have known of a work by a rabbi in another country, another language, and another time, and should have found his account of the situation of Jews in the "Fair City of Venice" (as the subtitle had it) so instructive for the Jews in England almost a century later. Toland was sufficiently moved by that book to announce his intention of translating it into English. A few years later, he wrote another book that went beyond his (and Luzzatto's) arguments about the salutary effects of the Jews in their respective countries. He then looked forward to a time when the Jews might be resettled, with the same fortunate results, in their own "Mosaic Republic."

> It will follow, that as the Jews known at this day, and who are dispersed over Europe, Asia, and Africa, with some in America, are found by good calculation to be more numerous than either the Spaniards (for example) or the French, so if they ever happen to be resettled in Palestine upon their original foundation, which is not at all impossible, they will then, by reason of their excellent constitution, be much more populous, rich, and powerful than any other nation now in the world. I would have you consider whether it might be not both the interest and duty of Christians to assist them in regaining their country.[20]*

Other Hebraists were equally enthusiastic, proposing the ancient "Hebrew Commonwealth" as the model for the English government. In 1740 the Nonconformist minister Moses Lowman published a *Dissertation on the Civil Government of the Hebrews in which the True Designs and Nature of Their*

---

* Toland was not so favorably disposed to all religions. To Catholics he was merciless. "We Britons," he wrote in another book, "further perceive that the governing principle of Rome is worldly, earthly, tyrannical; and that the papal hierarchy is a mere political faction, erecting a splendid, pompous, and universal empire over mankind."[21]

*Government Are Explained; The Justice, Wisdom and Good-
ness of the Mosaical Constitution Are Vindicated.* The title is
eulogistic enough, but the text is even more so.

> The Hebrew Commonwealth is, without question, one of
> the most ancient of the world, and justly looked upon as
> a model of government of divine origin; it will deserve our
> attention, as much as any of the forms of government in
> the ancient times, either among the Egyptians, Greeks, or
> Romans. It should more especially deserve our attention
> as Christians, who own the laws delivered by Moses to the
> Hebrew nation to have been given by the oracle of God,
> and established by authority of the supreme governor of the
> world; in which therefore, we may expect to find a wise and
> excellent model, becoming the wisdom of such a lawgiver.[22]

If the Jews had notable defenders, even venerators, in this
post-Lockean period, they also had their detractors, even vili-
fiers—and not only among zealous Christians with taunts of
Christ-killing, but among those who professed to be tolerant
and claimed tolerance for themselves. Many deists were hostile
to Judaism because that was theism's legacy to Christianity, and
contemptuous of Jews, in the present as in antiquity, because
they were the practitioners of that odious religion. Thomas
Morgan, in 1737, in a curiously entitled book, *The Moral Philosopher: In a Dialogue Between Philalethes a Christian Deist,
and Theophanes a Christian Jew*, ransacked the Old Testament
for evidence of everything that was hateful in Christianity and
found in Jewry everything that was odious to humanity. Having been "perfectly Egyptianized" in that benighted country,
the Jews had left it in a state "of gross ignorance, superstition,
and moral wickedness, which ran through all their successive
generations, till their final dissolution and destruction." The

law Moses gave them was arbitrary, being nothing more than the voice and will of God. Without any basis in nature, human wisdom, or prudence, it made no distinction between morals and rituals, thus leaving the Jews with a constitution that could "serve only to blind and enslave those that were under it."[23]

It was against this background—from "apathetic" or benign toleration, to enthusiastic philosemitism, interspersed with the familiar antisemitic outbursts—that the Jewish Naturalization Bill was introduced in 1753. Yet the discussion of the "Jew Bill," as it was generally known, was relaxed, muted, and for the most part impassionate.* The title was something of a misnomer. The bill applied not to Jews in general, but only to immigrants. Jews born in England were naturalized, so to speak, by birth. Whatever "disabilities" they had were those of all non-Anglicans who could not take the required religious oath; they could not hold municipal office, vote, sit in Parliament, or get a university degree. Jews born abroad, however, like all immigrants, were aliens and had additional disabilities, such as the inability to own land and engage in some forms of foreign trade. The Jew Bill was meant to equalize the status of Jews, giving immigrants the same rights and privileges—and disabilities—of native-born Jews.

There had been earlier attempts to solve the problem of all immigrants, non-Jewish as well as Jewish. In 1709 an act to naturalize foreign-born Protestants was passed, only to be repealed the following year. In the 1740s, the Irish Parliament considered, and rejected, bills for the naturalization of Irish Jews. At the same time, bills in the English Parliament for the naturalization of Protestants had to be withdrawn, in spite of

---

* The term "Jew Bill" was not meant invidiously. It was used by supporters and opponents of this bill as well as of the later ones.

the support of the Prime Minister Henry Pelham, because of strong opposition from the City. It is surprising, therefore, that the 1753 bill for the naturalization of English Jews was actually enacted—only to be repealed later that year.

The bill was simple enough. It provided that "persons professing the Jewish religion may, upon application for that purpose, be naturalized by Parliament without receiving the Sacrament of the Lord's Supper." In the House of Lords, the debate was brief, almost pro forma, and the bill was approved without a division on April 16. In the House of Commons the speeches were slightly more animated and overwhelmingly in favor of the bill. Only after the second reading did it begin to attract public attention; four petitions were sent to the Commons, two in favor and two against. The main objections were not religious but economic. A Whig pamphleteer favoring the bill deplored the self-serving motives of the opposition: "The conduct of the merchants who opposed the bill is easily accounted for: narrow principles, and a view to their private interests, were the incentive; they are disgusted at seeing the Jews trade in the same countries with them, and their trade would be more profitable, by there being fewer traders; never reflecting on the generous and certain maxim, that the most extensive trade is the most beneficial."[24]

The bill passed on May 22, by 96 votes to 55. While it was awaiting the royal assent, the public "clamor" (as it was always described) started.[*] It became a party issue on both economic and religious grounds. The Whigs had a more expansive view of trade (the more the better) and a more ecumenical (therefore tolerant) view of religion; the Tories a more restrictive view of

---

[*] It was also then that the phrase, "the Jewish question" was first used—not pejoratively, as it later was on the continent. In Europe in the nineteenth century, and more particularly in Germany (among the Young Hegelians, and Marx most notably), that expression had distinctly antisemitic overtones.[25]

trade and a more Erastian view of religion. Antisemitism did intrude itself, but it was less virulent than might be expected. Some of the objections were not to Jews specifically but to all foreigners (xenophobia was the basis for much antisemitism) and to all non-Anglicans (Catholics and Dissenters). The familiar slogan "Church and King" was modified to accomodate all these dissidents: "Church and King, without mass, meeting, or synagogue."[26] The Jews also had the misfortune of being identified with the Whigs, thus playing into the party struggle that occupied the public in the months before the parliamentary elections of 1754. "In the political vocabulary of 1753–54," one historian explains, "the words 'Jew' and 'Whig' became practically synonymous. . . . The 'anti-Jewish' clamor of 1753 was meant, even at its ugliest, to prepare the ground not for a pogrom, but for a general election."[27]

Even good churchmen were dismayed by the public outcry against the bill and by the supineness of politicians of both parties. In June, the Bishop of Oxford regretted that the bill "hath not only raised very great clamors amongst the ignorant and disaffected, but hath offended great numbers of better understandings and dispositions, and is likely to have an unhappy influence on the elections of the next year." But he too shamefacedly confessed the need to bow to "weak and misguided consciences."[28] A few months later, the Archbishop of Canterbury observed that "faction, working upon the good old spirit of High Church, has made wild work in the nation," going on, however, to explain that since the passage of the bill was "worth no hazard," the repeal of it was "hardly worth a debate."[29] Members of Parliament had no change of heart about the bill itself; they merely responded to the passions of the people "out-of-doors" (the public). Lord Hardwicke made the best of this unhappy situation:

However much the people may be misled, yet in a free country I do not think an unpopular measure ought to be obstinately persisted in. We should treat the people as a skilful and humane physician would treat his patient; if they nauseate the salutary draught we have prescribed, we should think of some other remedy, or we should delay administering the prescription till time or change of circumstances has removed the nausea.[30]

The act was was repealed in November, only six months after its passage, with hardly a debate and without a division in either House. Six months later, the Whigs were returned to Parliament with a comfortable margin. Almost immediately, passions subsided and the episode was over. In his memoirs, Horace Walpole (son of the former Prime Minister and himself a Member of Parliament) took the measure of the times and the issue. The repeal, he observed, "showed how much the age, enlightened as it is called, was still enslaved to the grossest and most vulgar prejudices." The act originally passed almost without comment, only two members of the House of Lords having given "a languid opposition to it, in order to reingratiate themselves with the mobs of London and Westminster." For the rest, the bishops had concurred in removing the absurd distinctions that "stigmatized and shackled a body of the most loyal, commercial, and wealthy subjects of the kingdom." But then politics took hold.

A new general election was approaching; some obscure men, who perhaps wanted the necessary sums for purchasing seats, or the topics of party to raise clamor, had fastened on this Jew Bill; and in a few months the whole nation found itself inflamed with a Christian zeal. . . . Indeed, this holy spirit seized none but the populace and the very lowest of the clergy: yet all these grew suddenly so zealous for the honor of the prophecies that foretell calamity and eternal dispersion to the Jews, that they seemed to fear lest the completion of them should be defeated by act of Parliament; and there wanted nothing to their ardor but to petition both Houses to enact the accomplishment. The little curates preached against the bishops for deserting the interests of the Gospels; and aldermen grew drunk at county clubs in the cause of Jesus Christ, as they had used to do for the sake of King James. Yet to this senseless clamor did the ministry give way; and to secure tranquility to their elections, submitted to repeal the bill.[31]

The Jew Bill and the protests against it were soon forgotten, by the public and even by Jews. The repeal was only nominally a defeat for the Jews because it left their legal status unchanged. The "clamor" was nothing more than that. There was no physical violence against Jews, no call for their expulsion or even demands for punitive measures against them. On the contrary, two other acts, on monopolies and marriage, passed in the same year as the ill-fated Jew Bill, contained specific exemptions in favor of the Jews. New Jewish immigrants remained aliens, but their English-born children were not. The Jewish community continued to grow and thrive, economically and socially. In the middle of the century, the Jews in England numbered 8,000, one-tenth of one percent of the English population, of whom about a half had been born abroad and most of whom lived in London. By the end of the century there were over 25,000, of whom about 5,000 were in the provinces.[32] When the naturalization issue was finally resolved in 1826, it was not in the form of a Jew Bill but by an act abolishing the sacramental test for all immigrants. There was no significant opposition, no public clamor, no singling out of the Jews for special commendation or disapprobation.

A dozen years after the abortive Jew Bill, Adam Smith (without mentioning it), commented on one of the objections that had been brought against the Jews: the "vulgar prejudice" against them as "traders." In his *Lectures on Jurisprudence*, Smith traced that prejudice back to those "rude ages" when people had a "mean and despicable" opinion of all merchants, and of Jews in particular who, because they were outlawed from other occupations, were disproportionately merchants. Even in the present "refined" age, that contempt for trade persisted, to the detriment of commerce and of society. The Jews especially "were grievously oppressed and consequently the progress of opulence greatly retarded."[33] "The progress of opulence"—on Smith's part, this was no mean tribute to Jews, for it connected them, by way of commerce, to the "opulence" of society, which is to say, the "wealth of the nation."[*]

Edmund Burke, a friend and disciple of Adam Smith, may appear to be a less plausible friend of Jews. His references in *Reflections on the Revolution in France* to "Jew brokers" and "money-jobbers, usurers, and Jews" are the classic rhetoric of antisemitism, as is his diatribe against Lord George Gordon—a "public proselyte to Judaism," heir to "the old hoards of the synagogue, . . . the long compound interest of the thirty pieces of silver."[35] In the case of Gordon, however, what provoked Burke was not his new-found Judaism but his role in fomenting

---

[*] There is no mention of Jews in *The Wealth of Nations*. But the memorable phrase, "the propensity to truck, barter, and exchange," was anticipated in Smith's *Lectures on Jurisprudence* in the context of the unfortunate prejudice against Jews. Commenting on merchants and Jews, he spoke of "that principle in the mind which prompts to truck, barter, and exchange, though it is the great foundation of arts, commerce, and the division of labor, yet is not marked with any thing amiable."[34]

the anti-Catholic riots of 1780, which resulted in the destruction of Catholic chapels and homes, the killing and wounding of almost five hundred people, and Gordon's conviction and imprisonment on the charge of high treason. Of his conversion to Judaism seven years later, Burke remarked that he was unworthy of the religion to which he had converted, and recommended that he "meditate on his Talmud, until he learns a conduct more becoming his birth and parts, and not so disgraceful to the ancient religion to which he has become a proselyte."[36]

Shortly after the Gordon riots, Burke had occasion to speak of Jews in quite a different context and spirit. In May 1781, he presented a motion in Parliament to inquire into the condition of Jews in the West Indies island of St. Eustatius, which the British had captured a few months earlier after yet another Anglo-Dutch war. The island had a substantial Jewish community, mainly merchants and plantation owners, and the British, upon taking possession of the area, had confiscated much of their property and ordered their deportation. The Jews appealed in vain to the new authorities and Burke vigorously supported them, urging the British Parliament to reverse their actions and to behave humanely and protectively to a much abused people.

> The persecution was begun with the people, whom of all others it ought to be the care and the wish of humane nations to protect, the Jews. Having no fixed settlement in any part of the world, no kingdom nor country in which they have a government, a community, and a system of laws, they are thrown upon the benevolence of nations, and claim protection and civility from their weakness, as well as from their utility. They were a people, who, by shunning the profession of any, could give no well-founded jealousy to any state. If they have contracted some vices, they are such as naturally arise from their dispersed, wandering,

and proscribed state. . . . Their abandoned state and their
defenceless situation call most forcibly for the protection of
civilized nations. If Dutchmen are injured and attacked, the
Dutch have a nation, a government, and armies to redress
or revenge their cause. If Britons are injured, Britons have
armies and laws, the laws of nations (or at least they once
had the laws of nations) to fly to for protection and justice.
But the Jews have no such power, and no such friend to
depend on. Humanity then must become their protector and
ally. Did they find it in the British conquerors of St. Eustatius? No. On the contrary, a resolution was taken to banish
this unhappy people from the island.[37]

It may go too far to call Burke a philosemite, yet this speech
might begin to qualify him as that, all the more because he chose
to take up the cause of the Jews on this occasion when appar-
ently no other Englishman did, and when it was not in his own
interest to do so. Jews would also have been well served by the
principle of toleration he advocated in the *Reflections*. Criticiz-
ing the French revolutionaries for confiscating the property of
the church and for undermining religion in the name of reason,
he accused them of perverting the idea of toleration.

We hear these new teachers continually boasting of their
spirit of toleration. That those persons should tolerate all
opinions, who think none to be of estimation, is a matter of
small merit. Equal neglect is not impartial kindness. The species of benevolence, which arises from contempt, is no true
charity. There are in England abundance of men who tolerate in the true spirit of toleration. They think the dogmas of
religion, though in different degrees, are all of moment. . . .
They favour, therefore, and they tolerate. They tolerate,
not because they despise opinions, but because they respect

justice. They would reverently and affectionately protect all religions, because they love and venerate the great principle upon which they all agree, and the great object to which they are all directed.[38]

From Locke to Burke—it was a momentous period in the history of English Jews, not because it witnessed any dramatic changes (the small eruption created by the Jew Bill was of no lasting consequence), but precisely because it was so undramatic and uneventful. Other groups did not fare so well. There were anti-Dissenter riots early in the century, anti-Irish riots in the 1760s, and the anti-Catholic Gordon riot in 1780, but no anti-Jewish riots. One historian suggests that anti-Catholicism may have helped "deflect a good part of the hostility that might have been directed at Anglo-Jewry."[39] But it might be also argued that one kind of riot may have whetted the appetite for others. If anti-Irish and anti-Catholic, why not anti-Jew? In fact, it was a relatively tranquil period for Jews of all classes, not only for the rich financiers and merchants who enjoyed the company of high society and literati (of Walpole, for example), but also for more lowly merchants and artisans who plied their trades peacefully, and even for the hawkers and peddlers who were often derided but rarely physically abused—above all, for all Jews who enjoyed complete freedom of worship.

This was all the more remarkable because there was a great influx of Jews into England after a wave of massacres in East Europe in 1768. By the end of the century the number of English Jews had increased more than threefold. Since most of the immigrants were poor, they brought with them the problems associated with poverty, including crime. A particularly heinous murder in 1771 by a band of Jewish criminals provoked antisemitic cries in the streets and some abuse of peddlers. The government responded by imposing a moderate limitation on Jewish immigration; the immigrants had, for example, to pay their passage in advance. The Aliens Act of 1793 (not, it is interesting, a "Jewish Aliens Act") put foreigners in England under stricter control, but gave the synagogues, not the magistrates, responsibility for the registration of Jews. A Seditious Meetings Bill two years later was modified so as not to penalize Jews. That year the Jewish financier and philanthropist Abraham Goldsmid raised a fund for an institution to ameliorate the condition of the Jewish poor. Of the eighty-seven initial subscribers, forty-one were Christians.[40]

Napoleon scoffed at the "nation of shopkeepers," anticipating their quick defeat in battle. But Smith, who invented that phrase (with no pejorative intent), would have known better—as did the Jewish shopkeepers, who appreciated the country that was treating them, for the most part, civilly and tolerantly. It remained for later generations of English Jews to seek something more than civility and toleration—political equality as well. This was the ultimate test for Jews who happened to be living in a Christian society, in a state with an established Church, and who had the misfortune to be engaged in occupations that were regarded as "odious."

It may be that the principle of toleration alone, rigorously applied, would have enabled Jews to pass that test. In the event, something else came to their aid, a respect, even admiration, for Judaism that was often tantamount to philosemitism. The two sentiments, toleration and philosemitism, were philosophically and temperamentally very different, even to a degree contradictory. Yet they worked together in harmony, as "fellow-travelers," so to speak, using different means to arrive at the same end.

III.

The Case for
Political Equality

In 1833, the Lord Chancellor, Lord Brougham, informed the House of Lords: "His Majesty's subjects professing the Jewish religion were born to all the rights, immunities, and privileges of His Majesty's other subjects, excepting so far as positive enactments of the law deprived them of those rights, immunities, and privileges."[1] This was the "Jewish question" that dominated the history of British Jews in the first half of the nineteenth century—the attempt to remove the exceptions, or "disabilities," as they were called, that deprived them of "those rights, immunities, and privileges." One of those disabilities was removed by the act of 1826 that eliminated the Sacramental requirement for all immigrants, restoring, in effect, the Jew Bill of 1753 without mentioning Jews. But subsequent measures alleviating the conditions of Dissenters and Catholics were less accommodating to Jews. The repeal in 1828 of the Test and Corporation Acts, requiring the Sacramental oath for all public offices, applied to Dissenters but not Jews; in its final version it retained the statutory oath of allegiance to the sovereign "on the true faith of a Christian." And the Catholic Relief Act the following year removed the restrictions on Catholics, giving them all the political rights enjoyed by Anglicans and Dissenters. That left only the Jews who were still deprived of those rights. They could, for example, serve as parish officers but not as municipal officers. A more serious anomaly was the fact that although they could normally vote for Members of Parliament on the same terms as other citizens (the technical requirement of a religious oath was rarely, if ever, observed), they could not sit in Parliament, which did require the oath.* The Jewish Board of Deputies, including such eminences as Isaac Goldsmid, Moses Montefiore, and Lionel Rothschild, enlisted the support of leading figures in both parties in a campaign to give Jews the same rights that Dissenters and Catholics now enjoyed.

On April 5, 1830, a bill "to repeal the civil disabilities affecting British-born subjects professing the Jewish religion" was introduced by Robert Grant, a Whig and prominent Evangelical (a founding member of the Philo-Judaean Society established a few years earlier). Reviewing the history of English Jewry, Grant recalled the persecution of that "unfortunate race" leading to their expulsion, their readmission under Cromwell and the favorable treatment they received under succeeding monarchs, the bill of 1753 which "by the miserable pusillanimity of the ministry" had been repealed, and the unwarranted disabilities under which they still labored. To the objection that the granting of political rights to Jews violated the Christian nature of the polity, Grant replied that the very foundations of Christian-

---

* Of the three required oaths for public office (and for other purposes, such as attendance in a university)—the oaths of Allegiance, Supremacy, and Abjuration—it was the last that was the hindrance for Jews. Allegiance to the monarch was no problem; nor was the recognition of the monarch as the Supreme Governor of the Church of England. The oath of Abjuration, however, originally intended to exclude pretenders to the throne, was a problem because it concluded with the words, "on the true faith of a Christian."[2]

ity were in the Jewish Scriptures and their emancipation was in the best interests of this "Christian kingdom."

> The Jews spoke, as it were, a universal language, and they would spread the story of British liberality in the remotest corners of the globe. Hitherto they had known Christianity only as the pretext for savage persecutions, and they would celebrate the change, not merely with empty praises, but with the solid advantage of commercial preference. How willingly would they contribute to the welfare and prosperity of a Christian kingdom, which, though tardily, had generously conferred benefits hitherto withheld.[3]

The rebuttal to Grant came, ironically, from another Evangelical, Robert Inglis, a Tory member from Oxford. Refuting Grant's argument that their small numbers (20,000 in London and 30–40,000 in the United Kingdom) would constitute no threat to Britain, Inglis cited Edmund Burke's observation that a small group could exercise an influence, and an unfortunate one, well beyond their numbers. (Burke had made that comment not about Jews but about any dissident minority.) It was the nature of the Jewish community, Inglis insisted, that was the problem.

> The Jews were aliens, not in the technical and legal sense, when Lord Coke called them "aliens and perpetual enemies," but in the popular sense of the word: they were aliens because their country and their interests were not merely different, but hostile to our own. The Jews of London had more sympathy with the Jews resident in Berlin or Vienna than with the Christians among whom they resided. . . . They were not a sect; but to this day they called themselves a people; and they might avail themselves of

their political influence for objects connected with their own aggrandisement.[4]

At this point in the debate, two members of Parliament stood up to speak in defense of the bill: Sir James Mackintosh, the philosopher, jurist, and perhaps leading Whig intellectual in Parliament, and Thomas Babington Macaulay, a young man who had just won a seat in the House. In accord with the custom of giving precedence to a new member, Macaulay was recognized first and went on to deliver his maiden address to the House of Commons. It is interesting that he chose this subject on this important occasion, rather than the larger issue of parliamentary reform, which might have made for a more dramatic entry into Parliament. (His speech on the Reform Bill the following year did just that, establishing him as an important presence in the House and a skillful orator.) Macaulay, then thirty years old, the son of the venerable Evangelical Zachary Macaulay, shared his father's spiritedness and talents (although not his religious zeal), and was already well known as an essayist and frequent contributor to the *Edinburgh Review*. Early that year, he offered to write an article on the bill that was being proposed. "The Jews," he wrote the editor of the *Review*, "are about to petition Parliament for relief from the absurd restrictions which lie on them—the last relic of the old system of intolerance. . . . I would gladly further a cause so good, and you, I think, could have no objection."[5]

Macaulay's speech in Parliament was a briefer version of the essay that was later to appear in the *Review*. The bill, he said, was based on the same principle of religious toleration as the Catholic Emancipation Act, and those who had opposed that act had less reason to oppose this one. "There is no foreign power to be feared. There is no divided allegiance threatening the state, . . . there is no priesthood exercising an absolute authority, . . . there are no agitators rousing and exciting the people." Unlike the Catholics, the Jews did not try to gain proselytes; they sought only to keep their religion for themselves. Nor did they engage in anything like the Gunpowder Plot or similar acts of violence committed by Catholics. On the contrary, the history of English Jews reveals the "wrongs suffered and injuries endured by them, without a trace of any wrong or injury committed in return; . . . atrocious cruelties inflicted on the one hand, and grievous privations endured for conscience sake on the other." All that was left of the opposition to their emancipation were the "offal," the "leavings" of intolerance left over from earlier years. The only remaining objection was that "the Jews are not Christians, and that therefore they must not have power." It was this argument that Macaulay turned against them by insisting that power, real power, was precisely the ground for the emancipation of the Jews.

> The only power that my hon. friend seems to wish to deprive the Jews of is to consist in maces, gold chains, and skins of parchment, with pieces of wax dangling at the ends of them. But he is leaving them all the things that bestow real power. He allows them to have property, and in these times property is power, mighty and overwhelming power. He allows them to have knowledge, and knowledge is no less power. Then why is all this power poisoned by intolerance? Why is the Jew to have the power of a principal over his clerk, of a master over his servant, of a landlord over his tenant? Why is he to have all this, which is power, and yet to be deprived of the fair and natural consequences of this power? . . . As things now stand, a Jew may be the richest man in England—he may possess the whole of London—his interest may be the

means of raising this party or depressing that—of making East-India directors, or sending members into Parliament— the influence of a Jew may be of the first consequence in a war which shall be the means of shaking all Europe to its centre. His power may come into play in assisting or retarding the greatest plans of the greatest Princes; and yet, with all this confessed, acknowledged, undenied, my hon. friend would have them deprived of power! If, indeed, my hon. friend would have things thus arranged, I would put a question to him thus:—Does he not think that wealth confers power? If it do, can he be prepared to say that the Jew shall not have power? If it do not, where are we to draw the line? How are we to permit all the consequences of their wealth but one?[6]

It was a novel and audacious argument, and could easily have had the opposite of the intended effect. To ascribe to Jews a considerable measure of wealth, and then to go on to assert that economic power naturally translated itself into political power, could confirm the worst suspicions and fears of antisemites. Indeed, it gave good reason to oppose the bill, to deny the Jews political power and even deprive them of some of their excessive and dangerous wealth. That the opponents of the bill did not respond to it in this fashion is itself a measure of the civililty of the debate. Macaulay himself, as if conscious of the unfortunate implications of his remarks, went on to change the tenor of his speech. Recalling the bad old days when Jews were persecuted, "when as a people they were pillaged, when their warehouses were torn down, when their every right was sacrificed," he now posed the issue not as a legal right to political power but as a moral right. To deprive them of that right on religious grounds alone was "as much persecution in principle as an *auto da fé*," the only difference being one of degree. A Parliament that had already passed important acts of religious liberty, he concluded, should put the finishing touch to those good works by passing this "most desirable measure."[7]

Parliament did not pass this "most desirable measure." It failed in the second reading by 228 to 165 votes. But Macaulay's maiden speech was a success. Mackintosh, who followed him, gracefully said that he could find no defect in it and spoke only to "absolve his own conscience."[8] The Jewish community was even more enthusiastic. Goldsmid gave a grand party for him in the House of Commons, which Macaulay reported on, in his usual jocular manner, to his sister the following day:

> I dined with a Jew,
> Such Christians are few,
> He gave me no ham,
> But plenty of lamb,
> And three sorts of fishes,
> And thirty made dishes.
> I drank his champagne
> Again and again . . . .
> O Christians whose feasts
> Are scarce fit for beasts,
> Example take you
> By this worthy old Jew.[9]

Macaulay's essay the following January in the *Edinburgh Review* raised some of the same themes as the speech but the emphasis was different. The point about money and power appeared more briefly and the ironic note was more obvious. "It would be impious to let a Jew sit in Parliament. But a Jew may make money; and money may make members of

Parliament. . . . That a Jew should be privy-councillor to a Christian king would be an eternal disgrace to the nation. But the Jew may govern the money-market, and the money-market may govern the world." The heart of the essay was the classic argument for toleration: the irrelevance of religion—Christianity as well as Judaism—to politics.

> We hear of essentially Protestant governments and essentially Christian governments, words which mean just as much as essentially Protestant cookery, or essentially Christian horsemanship. . . . The points of difference between Christianity and Judaism have very much to do with a man's fitness to be a bishop or a rabbi. But they have no more to do with his fitness to be a magistrate, a legislator, or a minister of finance, than with his fitness to be a cobbler. . . . What is proposed is not that the Jews should legislate for a Christian community, but that a legislature composed of Christians and Jews should legislate for a community composed of Christians and Jews.

After absolving Jews of the charge of being aliens or otherwise unfit for all the rights of Englishmen—if they were that it was only because the English had made them so—Macaulay concluded by rebuking the writer who claimed that it was a "monstrous indecency" to have introduced the bill during the Easter session with a possible second reading on Good Friday. Macaulay could think of no more fitting time than that holy day "for terminating long hostilities, and repairing cruel wrongs, . . . for blotting out from the statute-book the last traces of intolerance."[10]

Two years later, Macaulay spoke in favor of yet another bill in support of "that religion which first taught the human race the great lesson of universal charity."[11] This time the bill passed easily in Commons only to be rejected in the Lords, mainly because of the opposition of the bishops. The fate of similar bills in 1834 and 1836 was much the same, after which the subject was permitted to lapse for eleven years. But Macaulay's essay in the *Edinburgh Review*, often reprinted and widely circulated, helped keep the issue, and his role in it, alive.

Macaulay was not alone in unwittingly reinforcing the anti-semitic image of the Jew, even while supporting the bill and defending the Jews against just that image. An essay by William Hazlitt, written shortly before his death and published posthumously in the *Tatler* in March 1831, had the same ambiguous effect. Opening on an optimistic note—"The emancipation of the Jews is but a natural step in the progress of civilisation"—he concluded by urging people to get rid of the "vulgar prejudices" that were unworthy of them and by vindicating the Jews against those prejudices.

> If they are vicious it is we who have made them so. Shut out any class of people from the path to fair fame, and you reduce them to grovel in the pursuit of riches and the means to live. . . . The Jews barter and sell commodities, instead of raising or manufacturing them. But this is the necessary traditional consequence of their former persecution and pillage by all nations. . . . You drive them like a pest from city to city, from kingdom to kingdom, and then call them vagabonds and aliens.[12]

Hazlitt may have been provoked by William Cobbett, who shared the most vulgar of those prejudices. The "Poor Man's Friend," as Cobbett liked to think of himself, despised a great many people, including Evangelicals, Unitarians, Quakers, and Negroes, but Jews above all. It may have been Cobbett's pamphlet in 1830, "Good Friday; or the Murder of Jesus Christ by the Jews," that inspired Macaulay to insist that Good Friday was precisely the appropriate day for the passage of the bill, and that prompted Hazlitt to defend the Jews against the familiar prejudices. What enraged Cobbett was not only the Jew as Christ-killer but also the Jew as financier, merchant, money-lender, and usurer. (He habitually used the word "Jew" as synonymous with those activities.) He praised the rulers on the continent (the king of Prussia, for one) for their repressive policies towards the Jews, holding up to them as a model the persecutions in the Middle Ages. And he proposed that England follow the example of the Czar in expelling the Jews: "The banishment of the Christ-killers from Russia is really a proof to me that the Emperor of Russia is not a tyrant"—perhaps because the Czar merely had the Jews banished rather than killed.[13]

Thomas Carlyle, somewhat less virulent than Cobbett, shared his animus against Jews for much the same reasons. James Froude, Carlyle's friend and biographer, recalled standing with him on Hyde Park corner before the grand house of Rothschild. A latter-day monarch, Carlyle told Froude, might emulate what King John had done in 1210. When one Jew refused to pay the ransom that had been demanded of all Jews, the king had one of his teeth pulled out every day until that ransom had been paid. A more benign torture, perhaps a twist of the wrist, Carlyle suggested, might induce Rothschild to give up some of the millions he had nefariously acquired. Even Froude was taken aback by that not so facetious remark. Carlyle, he noted, had a "true Teutonic aversion for that unfortunate race."[14]

The "vulgar prejudices" Hazlitt complained of persisted well into the century, although in a milder manner. (Cobbett himself died in 1835, and with him went an especially rancorous mode of polemic.) The prejudices expressed themselves more often in private discourse than in public, and never in any organizational form. There was no League of Antisemites (as in Germany), no riots, and no government-sponsored or -sanctioned antisemitic acts or declarations. Instead, there was a growing sense of toleration and social acceptance, accompanied by small but significant measures of amelioration. In 1833, Isaac Goldsmid's son Francis was admitted to the bar, swearing on a Hebrew Bible. Two years later, the *de facto* situation became *de jure* when all oaths for voting were abolished. In 1836, the Jewish Board of Deputies was authorized to certify Jewish places of worship for purposes of marriage. The University of London founded that year (incorporating the previously established University College, London) was open to students and teachers of all religions. (Oxford and Cambridge remained barred to Jews until 1871.) In 1837, Moses Montefiore became sheriff of London and was knighted, the first Jew since 1700 to receive that honor.* Four years later, Isaac Goldsmid became the first Jew to be given the hereditary title of baronet. In 1845, a Jewish Disabilities Removal Act officially removed the mandatory oath for municipal offices. The following year, an act repealed earlier restrictive legislation (some dating back to Norman times and much of it not observed) concerning schools, charities, and places of worship.

In 1847, attention returned to the remaining conspicuous disability, the seat in Parliament, this time not as an abstract principle but as a practical matter. In the general election of that

---

* Five months after receiving his knighthood, Montefiore asked Russell to give him a baronetcy on the occasion of Queen Victoria's coronation. Among the attributes that qualified him, he said, were his fortune, a landed estate, and a "supreme attachment to the constitution." As if this would also be in his favor, he pointed out that since he had no children, the baronetcy would expire with him. In the event, that honor went not to him but to Goldsmid.[15]

year, Lionel de Rothschild, together with the Prime Minister, John Russell, were elected by the City of London as their representatives in Parliament. When Parliament met in December, Rothschild presented himself and explained that he could not take the religious oath. He was asked to withdraw, whereupon Russell moved that a committee of the House consider a bill for the removal of the civil and religious disabilities of Jews. The Jewish Disabilities Bill the following year (which focussed on the one disability, admission to Parliament) passed in the Commons by a comfortable margin—and was rejected in the Lords by an equally comfortable margin.

Although the fate of this bill was the same as the earlier ones, the debate on December 16th was more memorable, engaging some of the most prominent political figures, often in unpredictable ways. Russell's introductory defense was in the classic spirit of toleration. All native-born Englishmen were entitled to all "the honors and advantages of the British constitution." Anticipating the criticisms of Inglis, who was to follow him, Russell insisted that the entitlement was a matter of right, that religious opinions were no reason to deprive them of that right, and that the admission of Jews to Parliament would in no way undermine the integrity of the Christian nation and state. He also anticipated the familiar criticisms of Jews, citing Cobbett who had complained that they were not employed in "laborious occupations" or in the normal trades of most Englishmen. "But is there not a reason for that?" Russell asked. "What right have we to say, having forbidden them to hold land, or to engage in retail trades, you are disqualified because you show no disposition for acquiring land, and no industry in plying retail trades. Is that justice? Is that sound argument?"

"Justice" and "sound argument" in refutation of Cobbett, "right" and "birthright" in refutation of Inglis—that might have been enough in defense of the bill. But finally Russell returned to religion itself to vindicate an act that would have disqualified religion as the basis of membership in Parliament.

> I would make a still higher appeal—an appeal to the principles of Christianity, with which our laws are interwoven. I appeal to you in the name of that religion which is one of love and of charity, to do unto others as you would that others should do unto you. . . . I ask you then, in the name of that constitution, which is a constitution of liberty and of justice—I ask you in the name of that religion, which is a religion of peace and good-will towards men, to agree to the Motion which I have now the honour to make.[16]

The Liberal Prime Minister's speech was in the familiar liberal mode, echoing some of the arguments for toleration (although less provocatively) that Macaulay had advanced on the occasion of the first bill. He may have been surprised to find allies—reluctant ones, to be sure—among some Tories who had opposed the earlier bill. Sir Robert Peel, the Tory leader, supported this one on grounds not of justice or right but of consistency and expediency. Having already conceded the vote to Dissenters and Catholics, Peel reasoned, Parliament had to adapt to changing circumstances and grant the vote to Jews as well.

William Gladstone was a more surprising ally, making much the same argument as Peel (in whose cabinet he had served), although more tortuously and apprehensively. The member (with Inglis) of the Tory-minded constituency of Oxford, he had not only opposed the bill of 1833 as well as another that admitted Jews to municipal offices, but had written a book refuting the very principle of those bills. *The State in its Relations with the Church*, in 1838, was in the high-church Erastian tradition that assumed an identification of church and state, hence precluded the presence of Jews in Parliament, the political embodiment of the state.* To the dismay of his father and most of his constituents, and to his own discomfort, Gladstone now spoke in favor of Russell's motion. "It is a painful decision to come to," he wrote in his diary. And to his father, after delivering his speech, he explained: "It is with reluctance that I give the vote, but I am convinced that after the civil privileges we have given them [the Jews] already (including the magistracy and the franchise), and after the admission we have already conceded to Unitarians who refuse the whole of the most vital doctrines of the Gospel, we cannot compatibly with entire justice and fairness refuse to admit them."[17]

That one sentence sums up the long, labored speech Gladstone made in support of the measure that Inglis, his fellow-member from Oxford, vigorously opposed and that he knew his constituency did not favor. As a Member of Parliament, he told his electors, he represented them but had to abide by his own judgment and conscience, so that it was with deep regret and pain that he was now voting for the bill. He promised to be brief with regard to the "positive arguments" for the admission of Jews. And so he was, citing the praise of others attesting to the Jews' "powerful intellect, . . . their cultivated minds, . . . their ancient and continuous literature . . . , their indefatigable diligence . . . ." On his own, Gladstone added one more argument: "their intelligence and activity and success in many of the pursuits of commerce and of industry."

But all that was by way of aside. The burden of Gladstone's argument was the concessions that had already been made to others who failed the Church of England test. "It appears, then,

---

* More widely discussed than the book itself was the seventy-odd-page ruthless critique of it by Macaulay in the *Edinburgh Review* the following year.

we have now arrived at a stage in which, after two or three generations had contended for a Church Parliament, and two or three generations more contended for a Protestant Parliament, each being in succession beaten, we are called upon to decide the question whether we shall contend for a Christian Parliament." Gladstone's grudging answer was that the admission to Parliament of "an extremely small fraction of Jews," "a few solitary Jews," would not "nullify the Christianity" of the vast majority of other members and thus would not bring any "organic change in the connection between Church and State." He concluded, apologetically, by invoking the spirit of Christianity, which countenanced "an act of justice in spite of prepossessions appealing to our liveliest and tenderest feeling— prepossessions which still attracted our sympathy and respect, almost our veneration."[18]

It was a minimal, even, equivocal, "act of justice" that Gladstone invoked to counteract his natural "prepossessions"—the justice of giving the Jews what had already, unwisely and unjustly, been given to others. Jews had neither a legal nor a moral right to be in Parliament; they were to be there only because it would be a grievance to be excluded when everyone else was included. Moreover, they were to be included only on the assumption that there would be very few of them—and also recognizing that the "prepossessions" against them still held and were still worthy of sympathy and respect, almost "veneration." Disraeli, in his own speech later in the day, described Gladstone's speech as "politic." Gladstone disputed that characterization, insisting that he was reaffirming the principle that had governed his earlier votes as well as his book—the principle that Parliament would remain a Christian institution in a Christian State.

Disraeli's speech was to the opposite effect from Gladstone's, but it was no less strange, if only because it came from another Tory supporting a Whig measure that would have brought another Whig (Rothschild) into Parliament. In the light of their later careers, it is hard to remember that at this time Gladstone and Disraeli sat on the same side in the House. Yet even then they were as far apart as they would later be when they led their respective parties and opposed each other on virtually every issue. While Gladstone was trying to reconcile the bill with his treatise on church and state, Disraeli was approaching it in the light of the novel he had just published. "Half Christendom," the heroine of *Tancred* says, "worships a Jewess, and the other half a Jew. . . . Which do you think should be the superior race, the worshipped or the worshipper?"[19] Echoes of that novel, even the implicit answer to that question, may be heard in Disraeli's speech, which was as provocative as the novel itself.

Disraeli opened with an audacious proposition. The advocates of the bill favored it on the principle of religious liberty; the opponents objected to it on the principle of religious truth. He supported it for precisely the reason that others opposed it, because "there is something more excellent than religious liberty—and that more excellent thing is religious truth." And not only religious truth, but "religious truth taking the shape of religious conformity." The bill, he agreed with the opponents, was about religion, and more particularly about the Jewish religion.

> For who are these persons professing the Jewish religion.
> They are persons who acknowledge the same God as the
> Christian people of this realm. They acknowledge the same
> divine revelation as yourselves. They are, humanly speaking,
> the authors of your religion. They are unquestionably those
> to whom you are indebted for no inconsiderable portion
> of your known religion, and for the whole of your divine
> knowledge.

Interrupted by cries of outrage, Disraeli went on to offend members of both parties. If religious faith was a sanction for conduct, then surely those who "profess the religion which every gentleman in the House professes—for every gentleman here does profess the Jewish religion, and believes in Moses and the Prophets [again cries of protest]—well then, I say that if religion is a security for righteous conduct, you have that security in the instance of the Jews who profess a true religion." However degraded or brutalized a Jew might have become as a result of centuries of persecution, "he has been sustained by the divine law he obeys, and by the sublime morality he professes." It is as Christians, therefore, and in a Christian assembly, that Parliament should welcome the Jews. Others might support the bill on other grounds—of justice, expediency, or liberty. He was supporting it (again, to cries of protest) as a Christian, who could not exclude those "who are of the religion in the bosom of which my Lord and Savior was born."[20]

It was an extraordinary performance, not least because his audience was well aware of the fact that Disraeli, baptized as a child by his father, had been converted from that "true religion." They also knew that he had nothing to gain from that speech. Indeed, he had everything to lose by it. He was at a point in his career when he had to present himself to his Tory constituency and party as a "sound man," and there was already much about him that was unsound—his novels, his exotic appearance, and, of course, his Jewish heritage.[21] *Tancred* could be read as a fantasy, a *jeu d'esprit*—or "Jew *d'esprit*," as was said—but a parliamentary speech on an important occasion could not be so easily dismissed. However bizarre or outrageous it seemed to many at the time, it was, in fact, principled and heartfelt.

Another speech by another Tory, this time against the bill, also had its oddities, because it came from a man who in other respects was an ardent philosemite—indeed, a philo-Zionist. Lord Ashley (as he then was; a few years later he came into his title as the Seventh Earl of Shaftesbury) was an Evangelical best known for his championship of social reforms—factory, mining, and housing acts, schools for the poor, the abolition of slavery, and the like. But he was also engaged in Jewish causes, in protests against the persecution of Jews abroad, in societies for the conversion of Jews, and, most prominently, in the movement for the restoration of a Jewish holy land in Palestine.[22]

On this occasion, however, Ashley spoke up against the bill that would have completed the emancipation of Jews. Like Disraeli, but with the opposite intent, he argued that religion did indeed have "a great deal to do with politics." He quoted Macaulay derisively: "To talk of essentially Christian government is about as wise as to talk of essentially Protestant cookery, or essentially Christian horsemanship." This witticism was unworthy of that great genius, for if Christianity could not play a part in public life, "what was it that Christianity could do?" He also took issue with Russell who distinguished between the private and the public. Russell had admitted that "Christianity must prevail in private life," in which case, Ashley insisted, it must surely prevail in public life as well. Nor was Russell justified in saying that the exclusion of Jews "savored of persecution." The exclusion was based not on any personal objection to Jews but rather on a higher principle. Without that principle, why not admit "Mussulmans, Hindoos, and men of every form of faith under the sun in the British dominions"? Moreover, it was not probable but possible (this in response to Gladstone) that there might some day be in Parliament "a majority of the Hebrew nation, and that they might assume and retain the helm of affairs." In any case, to admit any Jews was to declare that "for all great public purposes Christianity was altogether needless."

It was at this point in his speech, very near the end, that Ashley suddenly launched into a passionate tribute to Jews—to modern Jews, not merely to the Jews of the Old Testament—which started almost as an apology and soon became an affirmation of philosemitism in its most extravagant form. He hoped, he said, that he had not given offense to "the Hebrew people," collectively or individually, for he himself regarded "the very poorest Israelite with feelings akin to reverence, as one of the descendants of the most remarkable nation that had ever yet appeared on the face of the earth." Others looked upon Jews as "a degraded, illiterate, money-loving race, fit only for the Stock Exchange or to take care of orange stalls." His view was quite the reverse.

> The Jews were a people of very powerful intellect, of cultivated minds, and with habits of study that would defy the competition of the most indefatigable German. Their literature extended in an unbroken chain from the days of our Lord down to the present time. ["From far beyond that," Disraeli interjected.] True, for the hon. Gentleman meant, no doubt, to throw into their literature the whole range of the historians and the prophets of the Old Testament. But he was speaking, not of the old Jews in their palmy days, but of the Jews oppressed and despised in their days of dispersion. Even thus, their literature embraced every subject of science and learning, of secular and religious knowledge. As early as the ninth century they took the lead in grammar and lexicography; and towards the end of the twelfth their labours in this respect formed the basis of everything that had since been done by Christian doctors. They had a most abundant literature in French and German, but especially in Hebrew; and the Jews presented, he believed, in our day, in proportion to their numbers, a far larger list of men of

genius and learning than could be exhibited by any Gentile
country. Music, poetry, medicine, astronomy, occupied their
attention, and in all they were more than a match for their
competitors. But the most remarkable feature in the character of the Jews in the present day was this, that they had
discarded very many of their extravagant and anti-social
doctrines. Their hatreds and their suspicions were subdued,
and undoubtedly they exhibited a greater desire and a
greater fitness to re-enter the general family of mankind.

Why then, he concluded, did he not support the present
measure in favor of that extraordinary people? He was prepared to make every concession that would contribute to "their
honour and comfort." But he could not acquiesce in striking
out from the oath the words that asserted the truth and the
supremacy of the Gospel, "on the true faith of a Christian."[23]

The 1847 bill elicited the most thoughtful, moving, and
sometimes paradoxical debate on both sides of the issue. But the
result was the same as the other bills—passage in the House and
rejection in the Lords. And so it went with the half-dozen later
bills that attempted to compromise on the wording and application of the oath. The formulation of the oath was a problem
for some Liberals as well as Tories. It might have been expected
that John Stuart Mill, the preeminent liberal philosopher of the
time, would have spoken out in favor of the bill. Instead the
only public comment he made, in a newspaper article in March
1849, was to criticize the bill introduced by Russell because it
was not liberal, not inclusive enough. By proposing to retain
the oath "upon the true faith of a Christian" for all Members
of Parliament except Jews, it had the effect of excluding "unbelievers." "He opens the door of parliament," Mill complained,
"just wide enough to allow one particular class of dissenters

to slip in and closes it, as far as depends upon him, against all others. . . . Were Hume and Gibbon improper persons to sit in Parliament?"[24]*

Not until July 26, 1858, when Rothschild stood for Parliament again, was yet another bill introduced which, after several amendments (and no very memorable speeches), the Lords reluctantly accepted. That bill empowered either House to alter the form of the oath for a member who objected to the traditional wording, "upon the true faith of a Christian." Rothschild then took his seat in the House of Commons, wearing a hat (in accordance with Jewish custom but in contravention of English), and swearing the oath "So help me Jehovah" on a large Hebrew Bible. That was not quite the end of the story, however, for that bill provided only for the particular Jew who chose the new oath—in this case, Rothschild. Two years later a further modification converted the exceptional case into a standing order applied to all Jews. Another act in 1866 prescribed for all members a shortened oath concluding with the words "So help me God," taken on either the Old or the New Testament. (This was waived for Quakers who could merely "affirm" without an oath or Bible.) Five years later, yet another bill removed the one remaining Jewish disability; a Jew could now be appointed Lord Chancellor.

---

* Mill was generally equivocal on the subject of religion. In his *Considerations on Representative Government*, he seemed to favor the people of the book over Christians because their book recognized the sacred character of the prophets. And because the prophets were often in opposition to their kings and priests, they provided that "antagonism of influences" that was the only security for progress and liberty—"the equivalent," he quoted one Hebrew commentator approvingly, "of the modern liberty of the press." Thus "the Jews, instead of being stationary like other Asiatics, were, next to the Greeks, the most progressive people of antiquity, and, jointly with them, have been the starting-point and main propelling agency of modern civilization."[25]

In his diary before that critical vote in 1858, Shaftesbury, then in the House of Lords, explained why he was going to reverse himself and vote for the measure he had so vigorously opposed a decade earlier. He could no longer resist, "pertinaciously and hopelessly," the will of the Commons. "I yield to force, not to reason. . . . More opposition is therefore futile."[26] Ten years later, he recalled that event to Gladstone, who had just succeeded Disraeli as prime minister. "The Jewish question has now been settled," he reminded him; Jews could now sit in both houses of Parliament. He himself had opposed their admission not because he was "adverse to the descendants of Abraham, of whom our Blessed Lord came according to the flesh," but because he objected to the mode in which that admission was effected. But all that, he said, was of the past. He now implored Gladstone to take the opportunity to show regard for "God's ancient people" by giving a peerage to "a noble member of the House of Israel," Sir Moses Montefiore. "It would be a glorious day for the House of Lords when that grand old Hebrew were enrolled on the lists of the hereditary legislators of England."[27]

It is ironic that Shaftesbury should be urging Gladstone to elevate Montefiore to the Lords, having once denied Rothschild a seat in the Commons. It is also ironic that he had made the same suggestion earlier to Disraeli when he was Prime Minister, only to be refused because Disraeli felt it would be unseemly for him, because of his heritage, to act on it. Gladstone, who had no such excuse and without explanation, also failed to do so, after inquiring, however, about the size of Montefiore's fortune and whether he had children (he did not). Montefiore who had been knighted in 1837, never received a peerage; he died in 1885 at the age of a hundred and one. Nor did Lionel Rothschild, who had not been knighted and had been proposed for a peerage in 1858 but was rejected by the Queen; in 1885 his son Nathan became the first Jew to sit in the House of Lords. The final irony is that Lionel Rothschild, having fought so hard and so long for a seat in Parliament, and having achieved that historic goal, spent fifteen years in the House without making a single speech.

In two centuries, the "Jewish question" had evolved from the question of the admission of Jews to England to that of the admission of Jews to Parliament. The resolution of both issues had much in common; they came about gradually, incrementally, civilly, by way of compromise and conciliation. They differed, however, in the quality of debate they engendered. The Jew Bills of the nineteenth century (as they were referred to) were the occasion for memorable speeches by eminent Victorians, which reveal a political and social ethos strikingly different from that on the continent.

Other countries in Europe had granted full political rights to Jews earlier in the century, but it was often against the background of impassioned popular antisemitism, or, as in Germany, the sophisticated antisemitism of philosophers and intellectuals. Moreover, the emancipation was generally granted under conditions, tacit or overt, that were demeaning to the very Jews who were being emancipated. Revolutionary France is generally credited with being the first European power to emancipate the Jews, but it did so at some cost. In the debate in the National Assembly, Mirabeau, one of the most moderate revolutionaries, declared that a Jew could be a citizen only if he was more *un homme* than a Jew. On that basis, the Assembly granted "active citizenship" only to the more assimilated Sephardi Jews. After another debate, in which the more observant Ashkenazi Jews were accused of being "a nation within a nation," they were given citizenship on the understanding that they would disavow their "Jewish corporations" and be admitted not as Jews but as individuals. "Jews as individuals," the supporter of the motion put it, "deserve everything; Jews as a nation nothing."[28]

In England, when Rothschild was admitted to Parliament, he did so as a Jew as well as a "man," taking the oath to the God of Israel on a Hebrew Bible. This was all the more notable because the issue was not, in fact, "citizenship," as defined by the franchise. It was more serious than that. Jews in England had long had the right to vote. What they did not have was the right to sit in Parliament. This was especially a problem in a country with an established Church, which presented a serious constitutional obstacle to the seating of Jews in the legislature. Jews were seeking admission not only to a secular society, not only to a Christian society, but to a Christian state as well. That they now achieved that goal was all the more memorable.

Twenty-five years earlier, Thomas Arnold, the master of Rugby, had vigorously opposed the admission of Jews to Parliament for precisely that reason. Protesting against the "low Jacobinical notion of citizenship," that a man acquires a right to it by the accident of birth or the payment of taxes, he declared England a Christian country where only Christians had a claim to political rights. Thus Catholics and Nonconformists who were Christians might be deemed citizens, but not Jews: "The Jews are strangers in England, and have no more claim to legislate for it than a lodger has to share with the landlord in the management of his house."[29]

His son Matthew Arnold surely intended no disrespect to his father (he may not have known of his father's views on that subject) when he refuted that argument, in effect, thirty-five years later in his memorable essay "Hebraism and Hellenism." His own preference, at least at that time and place, was for Hellenism, "right thinking," rather than Hebraism, "right acting." But both were integral parts of the English heritage and culture, knitting together "the genius and history of us English, and our American descendants across the Atlantic, to the genius and history of the Hebrew people."[30] In the preface to *Culture and Anarchy*, which included that essay, Arnold went further in distinguishing himself from his father. Jews, more than Nonconformists, were deserving of citizenship, because only within an establishment could the human spirit be cultivated. Nonconformists, lacking any establishment of their own and rejecting the very principle of an establishment, could produce no "men of national mark." Jews and Catholics, however, could produce such men because both rested on establishments—not national establishments, to be sure, but cosmopolitan ones.[31] The preface concludes with a tribute to Hebraism, which alone can give men "the happiness of doing what he knows." That is "the last word for infirm humanity." And for that word "our race will, as long as the world lasts, return to Hebraism; and the Hebrew Bible, which preaches this word, will forever remain, as Goethe called it, not only a national book, but the Book of the Nations."[32]

A few years earlier, Arnold anticipated some of the theme of "Hebraism and Hellenism" in an essay on Heinrich Heine. He then eulogized a converted Jew who remained, in heart and mind, faithful to the "race" he so brilliantly exemplified.

> His race he treated with the same freedom with which he treated everything else, but he derived a great force from it, and no one knew this better than he himself. He has excellently pointed out how in the sixteenth century there was a double renaissance—a Hellenic renaissance and a Hebrew renaissance—and how both have been great powers ever since. He himself had in him both the spirit of Greece and the spirit of Judaea; both these spirits reach the infinite, which is the true goal of all poetry and all art—the Greek spirit by beauty, the Hebrew spirit by sublimity. By his perfection of literary form, by his love of clearness, by his love

of beauty, Heine is Greek; by his intensity, by his untam-
ableness, by his "longing which cannot be uttered," he is
Hebrew.[33]

Arnold went on to quote Heine extensively on Jews and
Judaism: first, a moving story of a simple man, a Moses Lump,
who had all the dignity and self-esteem of a Rothschild; and
then long passages from Heine's poem on Jehuda Halevy. Today
that poem, in Heine's series called *Hebrew Melodies*, is one of
the classic texts in the literature of Zionism. Twenty years later,
a verse from another poem in this series, "Princess Sabbath,"
which Arnold had quoted in English, appeared in German as
an epigraph to one of the chapters in George Eliot's *Daniel
Deronda*.[34]*

From Thomas Arnold to Matthew Arnold—that one generation symbolized the change in the prevailing attitude toward
Jews, their acceptance as full citizens with all the rights and
privileges of Englishmen, and, at the same time, with all the
rights and privileges of Jews. These years also saw the full artic-
ulation of the ideas that were often latent or partially expressed
in earlier discussions of the "Jewish question." These ranged
from the classic liberal principle of toleration, to the prudent
acquiescence in political reality, to the most exuberant expres-
sions of philosemitism. At the very least what they reveal is a
strong countervailing force to antisemitism, a conscious, positive recognition of Jews as individuals as well as citizens—and,
in fiction especially, of Jews as a people, and, ultimately, as a
nation.

---

* Eliot herself had written a long adulatory essay on Heine some years earlier, but, oddly
enough, had made little of his Jewishness.

IV.

Fictional Heroes and Heroines

"The preeminent authors of the English literary canon, are Chaucer, Shakespeare, and Dickens. . . . They are also the preeminent authors of the English literary antisemitic canon." This dictum, by the historian Anthony Julius, is a sobering thought. We may be comforted by his reminder that the literary canon does not necessarily coincide with the social reality, that a nation may have "a rich *literary* antisemitism and a meager *political* antisemitism."[1] Yet the literary canon has a reality of its own, as is evident from the fact that two of these preeminent literary antisemites were living in England at a time when there were no Jews there. (In Shakespeare's day, there were a few Portuguese Marranos who were not publicly identified as Jews, the most notorious being the Queen's physician Rodrigo Lopez, who was accused of treason and publicly executed.) This is all the more reason to take seriously the fictional stereotypes that may be more dramatic and, in a sense, more real than the actual persons being caricaturized.

It is all the more reason, too, to be impressed by the emergence in the nineteenth century of a counter-canon, a philosemitic literary canon, so to speak, featuring admirable, even heroic Jews. These "counter-myths," as Lionel Trilling called them[2]—a new set of stereotypes, a cynic might say—did not dislodge the old, but they did create plausible alternative images which reinforced the philosemitism playing itself out in the political arena. The most striking exemplars of the new genre are novels by three of the best-known novelists of the period, Walter Scott's *Ivanhoe*, Benjamin Disraeli's *Tancred*, and George Eliot's *Daniel Deronda*—with Disraeli as a prime player in both the literary and political worlds.

Ivanhoe

In 1817, two years before the publication of *Ivanhoe*, Walter Scott commented on a novel he had just read, *Harrington*, by the Anglo-Irish novelist Maria Edgeworth.[*] The novel was delightful, Scott told a friend, but the subject left him with some misgivings.

> Jews will always be to me Jews. One does not naturally or easily combine with their habits and pursuits any great liberality of principle although certainly it may and I believe does exist in many individual instances. They are money-makers and money-brokers by profession and it is a trade which narrows the mind. I own I breathed more freely when I found Miss Montenero was not an actual Jewess.[3]

Miss Montenero, the daughter of a rich Jew of Spanish descent, is the fiancée of Harrington, the hero of the novel. Har-

---

[*] This fictional Harrington has no relation to James Harrington, the author of *Oceana*.

rington had been raised by a nursemaid who terrified him with stories of Jews who steal and slaughter children and use their blood for their rituals. As an adult he met and befriended real Jews, so that he is quite prepared to fall in love with the beautiful Miss Montenero. That love was fated to be unconsummated (his parents would never approve his marriage with a Jew) until her father tells him that she has been brought up as a Protestant in accord with the wishes of her mother, the daughter of an English (and Christian) gentleman. Thus Miss Montenero, "not an actual Jewess," is happily wedded to Harrington. Edgeworth, like Scott, presumably "breathed more freely" by relieving her heroine from the taint of Judaism. Yet the novel has an unmistakeably philosemitic tone, Mr. Montenero, an actual Jew, being entirely likeable, even admirable, as are other Jewish characters in the novel.[*]

Ivanhoe, set against a more dramatic historical background—late-twelfth-century England at the time of the Crusades—gives rise to the same potential misalliance. Unlike Edgeworth, however, Scott retained his heroine, Rebecca, as very much an "actual Jewess," by choice as well as birth. Indeed, she is all the more a heroine for resisting the temptation to convert or even to become the Templar's "paramour," which would have saved her from imminent death. This meant, however, that Scott, uneasy with that intermarriage, had to marry off his hero, the Saxon Ivanhoe, to Rowena, a good, if boring, Saxon lady. Scott may have "breathed more freely" with this denouement, but his readers did not, for it clearly violated their expectations as well as the romantic spirit of the novel.

---

* These agreeable Jewish characters were deliberate on the author's part. She was moved to write *Harrington*, her father explained in the preface to the novel, by an American Jewish lady who complained of the stereotypical Jews in her earlier stories and asked her to write a romance with a good Jew in it.

"Jews will always be to me Jews," Scott had said—and so they were in *Ivanhoe*. Rebecca's father, Isaac, is one of those "money-makers and money-brokers" whose profession "narrows the mind." He is also, however, capable of a "liberality of principle" that makes him a worthy father of Rebecca, willing to sacrifice himself, and his fortune, for her. He is not, to be sure, the hero of the novel—Ivanhoe is that—but he is far more commendable than most of the Saxons and Normans who behave ignobly toward each other and inhumanly toward Jews. It is a Knight Templar, Rebecca's unsuccessful suitor, who protests: "Will future ages believe that such stupid bigotry ever existed!"[4] Isaac makes his first appearance in a chapter introduced by an epigraph that is the classic expression of bigotry and an intimation of its injustice. "Hath not a Jew eyes? Hath not a Jew hands, organs, dimensions, affections, passions?"[5]

Where Edgeworth associated that bigotry with the blood-libel myth, Scott focused on the unrelieved history of oppression and persecution suffered by Jews. The facts are so horrendous that the author interrupts his narrative to insist that what he is describing is not fiction but historical fact:[*] "It is grievous to think that those valiant barons, to whose stand against the crown the liberties of England were indebted for their existence, should themselves have been such dreadful oppressors, and capable of excesses contrary not only to the laws of England, but to those of nature and humanity." A long quotation from the *Saxon Chronicle* depicts the torture inflicted by the Saxons upon the poor and the innocent. "They suffocated some in mud,

---

[*] Scott defended his blend of history and romance in the preface to the first edition of the book, a "Dedicatory Epistle to the Rev. Dr. Dryasdust, F.A.S." (In later editions it sometimes appears as an appendix.) Anticipating the objections of the antiquarian Dryasdust, Scott insisted that his was "a true picture of old English manners" based on true historic sources, although couched in modern language and perhaps taking some liberties with dates and facts.[6]

and suspended others by the feet or the head, or the thumbs, kindling the fire below them. They squeezed the heads of some with knotted cords till they pierced their brains, while they threw others into dungeons swarming with serpents, snakes, and toads" . . . and so on, in excrutiating detail.[7] Earlier in the novel, Isaac, escorted through the woods by an obliging pilgrim, suspects that he is being ambushed.

> His doubts might have been indeed pardoned; for, except perhaps the flying fish, there was no race existing on the earth, in the air, or the waters, who were the object of such an unintermitting, general, and relentless persecution as the Jews of this period. Upon the slightest and most unreasonable pretences, as well as upon accusations the most absurd and groundless, their persons and property were exposed to every turn of popular fury; for Norman, Saxon, Dane, and Briton, however adverse these races were to each other, contended which should look with greatest detestation upon a people, whom it was accounted a part of religion to hate, to revile, to despise, to plunder, and to persecute. The kings of the Norman race, and the independent nobles, who followed their example in all acts of tyranny, maintained against this devoted people a persecution of a more regular, calculated, and self-interested kind.[8]

It was in response to this unremitting persecution that the Jews developed the character traits they did. Their "obstinacy and avarice" increased in proportion to the "fanaticism and tyranny" to which they were subject. "On these terms they lived; and their character, influenced accordingly, was watchful, suspicious, and timid—yet obstinate, uncomplying, and skilful in evading the dangers to which they were exposed." It was thus that they not only survived but "increased, multiplied, and accumulated huge sums."* The Jews are aware of this double-edged nature of their existence. While they are being wronged, plundered, and derided, Isaac complains to his daughter, they have to "smile tamely" rather than "revenge bravely." Rebecca reassures him: "These Gentiles, cruel and oppressive as they are, are in some sort dependent on the dispersed children of Zion, whom they despise and persecute. Without the aid of our wealth, they could neither furnish forth their hosts in war nor their triumphs in peace; and the gold which we lend them returns with increase to our coffers."[10]

That struggle for survival had other fortunate effects. All the trials and tribulations to which Isaac and Rebecca are subject—extortions of wealth, accusations of witchcraft and sorcery, imprisonment, physical torment, and, finally, Rebecca's decree of death—give evidence of their fortitude and dignity. When Isaac is thrown into the dungeon, he is more composed than another might be: "Above all, he had upon his side the unyielding obstinacy of his nation, and that unbending resolution with which Israelites have been frequently known to submit to the uttermost evils which power and violence can inflict upon them, rather than gratify their oppressors by granting their demands."[11] So, too, when Rebecca and Rowena are imprisoned, with Rebecca in far greater peril than the Saxon lady, she has the advantage of being better prepared, "by habits of thought and by natural strength of mind," to confront the danger. "Like Damocles at his celebrated banquet," Rebecca

---

* Scott points out (again, with an unintentionally ambiguous effect), that in the course of amassing this wealth, the Jews invented a device for which commerce is "indebted to them": the bill of exchange, which permitted them to transfer their wealth from one country to another, so that "when threatened with oppression in one country, their treasure might be secured in another."[9]

beheld "the sword which was suspended over the heads of her people by a single hair."[12]

While persecution is a dominant theme in the book, religion is a relatively minor one. It is not God but the "obstinacy of his nation" that fortifies Isaac in the dungeon. And the "habits of thought" and "strength of mind" that prepare Rebecca for adversity come not from God but from the peril to which "her people" have always been subject. On the few occasions when God is invoked, it is almost as an afterthought. Seeking Rowena's help, she appeals to a Judaic-Christian God, "the God whom they both worshipped, and . . . that revelation of the Law upon Mount Sinai in which they both believed."[13] Later, finding herself without a defender before the "trial by combat" that will determine her fate, Rebecca is confident that "God will raise me up a champion." The Templar who has pity on her puts the question she might have asked of herself: "What has the law of Moses done for thee that thou shouldest die for it?" To which she replies: "It was the law of my fathers; it was delivered in thunders and in storms upon the mountain of Sinai, in cloud and in fire."[14] The only memorable act of piety occurs while she is awaiting the duel, when she recites the traditional evening prayer and sings a devotional hymn.[15] In the final scene, announcing her departure from England, she explains to Rowena (then married to Ivanhoe) that England is "no safe abode for the children of my people," no place where "Israel [can] hope to rest during her wanderings." Rowena begs her to remain in England where she can be weaned from her "erring law." No, Rebecca replies, "I may not change the faith of my fathers like a garment unsuited to the climate in which I seek to dwell. . . . He to whom I dedicate my future life will be my comforter, if I do His will." Is she going to retire to a convent? Rowena asks. No, Israel has no convents. She will do, as Jewesses always have done, devote "their thoughts to Heaven, and their actions to works of kindness to men." In parting, she commends Rowena to the God "who made both Jew and Christian."[16]

In his 1830 introduction to a new edition of *Ivanhoe*, Scott acknowledged the great success of the book and confronted some of the questions that had been raised about it. Like his other novels, this had been published anonymously; he now confessed that the author of the much-acclaimed Scottish-centered Waverley novels was also the author of this Anglo-Saxon novel. Addressing the complaints of those "fair readers" who objected to Ivanhoe's marriage to the "less interesting Rowena" rather than the "fair Jewess," he explained that "the prejudices of the age rendered such an union almost impossible"—echoing the scene in the novel when Ivanhoe, although attracted to Rebecca, resists her charm because he shares "the universal prejudices of his age and religion."[17] That they do not marry now appears as a point in Rebecca's favor, confirming her moral superiority not only over the prejudices of the age but also over the debasing instincts of self-gratification.

> A character of a highly virtuous and lofty stamp is degraded rather than exalted by an attempt to reward virtue with temporal prosperity. Such is not the recompense which Providence has deemed worthy of suffering merit. . . . A glance on the great picture of life will show that the duties of self-denial, and the sacrifice of passion to principle, are seldom thus remunerated; and that the internal consciousness of their high-minded discharge of duty produces on their own reflections a more adequate recompense, in the form of that peace which the world cannot give or take away.[18]

On that lofty note, "the sacrifice of passion to principle," Scott concluded his belated introduction, and Rebecca emerges as even more of a moral heroine than one might have thought, precisely because she is not married to the hero. What Scott did not say was what he had said in the novel, that the marriage had a larger significance than the union of man and wife. Attended by noble Saxons and Normans, the elaborate nuptials are "a pledge of the future peace and harmony betwixt the two races."[19] This marriage between the "two races," Saxon and Norman, was so successful that the distinction between them is now invisible. Left out of the marriage, of course, is that other "race," the Jews. For them there is no "peace and harmony." On the contrary, Rebecca and Isaac feel obliged to leave England to seek refuge abroad—an ominous anticipation of the expulsion of the Jews a century later.

Ivanhoe was even more successful than the Waverley novels. It sold ten thousand copies in the three-volume edition in a fortnight and remained a bestseller throughout the century. Six plays based on it appeared within a year of its publication and many more in later years, as well as several operas, including one by Rossini (which Scott saw in Paris in 1826 and complained that the story was mangled and the dialogue nonsense). In 1849, Thackeray published a spoof, *Rebecca and Rowena*, with Rowena a shrew jealous of her husband's feelings for Rebecca, and Ivanhoe, something of a drunkard, going off to fight for Richard. Eventually, after Rowena's death, he is free to marry Rebecca. But even that marriage is melancholic. "I think," the final sentence reads, "these were a solemn pair and died rather early."[20] "Solemn" or not, Rebecca the Jewess is unquestionably the heroine of the parody. Scott may have thought it inappropriate to have her marry Ivanhoe, but Thackeray did not. Nor did their readers. A Jewess, proud and resolute in her Jewishness, was thought to be a fit spouse for the hero, a Christian and a veteran of the Crusades.

If *Ivanhoe* belongs to the genre of the philosemitic novel, it is not the familiar mode of philosemitism. Judaism itself—its sacred texts, revered ancestors, rites and rituals—hardly figures in it. Nor is there any suspicion in the novel (or, for that matter, in Scott's life) of anything like the Hebraism, millenarianism, or veneration for the Old Testament that motivated other philosemites.* It is Rebecca's character, her determination to remain Jewish rather than the specific substance of that Jewishness, that qualifies her as the heroine of the novel, even as it disqualifies her as Ivanhoe's wife. So, too, it is the character of the Jewish people, nobly rising above oppression and persecution, that gives the novel its distinctively philosemitic tone.

Tancred

In *Ivanhoe*, the Templars are returning from the Third Crusade after attempting to recapture Jerusalem from the Muslims. In *Tancred*, more than six centuries later, an English gentleman goes to Jerusalem for "The New Crusade" (the subtitle of the book), not for conquest but to explore "the great Asian mystery" that has eluded Christianity all those years.

In 1844, when Disraeli published the first of his trilogy of novels, of which *Tancred* was the third, he had been in Parliament for seven years, had written a dozen novels, half-a-dozen political tracts, and delivered countless speeches. *Coningsby* was his political testament, a repudiation of the Tweedledum-

---

* In his last weeks, in a moment of consciousness, Scott requested his friend (and biographer) John Lockhart to read to him. "What book?," Lockhart asked. "Need you ask?" Scott replied. "There is but one." One historian cites this as evidence of Scott's interest in the Hebrew Bible. But it was a chapter of St. John's Gospel that Lockhart read to him, and it was this, Scott said, that was "a great comfort" to him.[21]

Tweedledee characters (the Peelite Conservatives) who had captured the Tory Party and were reducing it to a party of "Tory men and Whig measures." The "New Generation" of the subtitle was the Young Englanders who sought to preserve the venerable institutions of Crown and Church.* If *Coningsby* was the prototype of the political novel, *Sybil*, the following year, was the archetype of the social novel. Carlyle coined the phrase, "the condition-of-the-people-question," but it was Disraeli who publicized and dramatized it under the slogan, "The Two Nations," the subtitle of *Sybil*.

The last of the trilogy, *Tancred: The New Crusade*, was the spiritual part of the trilogy. It appeared in March 1847, nine months before Disraeli's memorable speech on the admission of Jews to Parliament. Two years later, he wrote a preface to the fifth edition of *Coningsby* that would have been more appropriate in *Tancred*. Reflecting upon the proper nature of Toryism, he saw the Church as the instrument for the "renovation of the national spirit." He was then moved to "ascend to the origin of the Christian Church"—Judaism.

> The modern Jews had long labored under the odium and stigma of medieval malevolence.... The Jews were looked upon in the middle ages as an accursed race, the enemies of God and man, the especial foes of Christianity. No one in those days paused to reflect that Christianity was founded by the Jews; that its Divine Author, in his human capacity, was a descendant of King David; that his doctrines avowedly were the completion, not the change, of Judaism.... The time had arrived when some attempt should be made to do justice to the race which had founded Christianity."[23]

---

* Just as Thackeray had written a spoof of *Ivanhoe*, so he wrote one of *Coningsby* under the title *Codlingsby*, mocking one of the characters who finds Jews in control everywhere: "Even the Pope in Rome is one of us."[22]

That "race" first appears in *Coningsby* in the person of Sidonia. The aristocrat Coningsby is inspired by a stranger to defy the wishes of his grandfather and undertake the difficult task of national renovation. The stranger, Sidonia, is also an aristocrat, but of a different order, a scion of that "unmixed race," the "aristocracy of Nature."[24] Descended· from a "very ancient and noble family of Arragon," the *Nuevos Christianos* (Marranos) who had secretly practiced their Jewish faith before being exiled, Sidonia made his fortune during the Napoleonic wars and emigrated to England where he could openly profess his faith.[*] It is there that he meets Coningsby, infecting him with the ideals that would transform English politics.

Sidonia reappears in *Tancred*, bearing the message "All is race; there is no other truth."[25] Like Coningsby, Tancred (Lord Montacute), the only son of the Duke of Bellamont, finds himself at odds with the political establishment, including his own father.[†] Repelled by the materialistic, soulless culture in England, he refuses to enter Parliament, telling his bewildered father that he wants instead to make a pilgrimage to the Holy Land, the "sepulchre of my Saviour," to find out "what is Duty, and what is Faith? What ought I to Do and what ought I to Believe?"[27] A family friend suggests that he call upon Sidonia, the famous Jewish banker, who might show him the inadvisability of that plan. "I am born in an age and in a country," Tancred informs

---

[*] Sidonia is generally said to have been modeled on Lionel Rothschild. The Rothschilds, however, were not Sephardim descended from the "Nuevos Christianos of Arragon." It was Disraeli himself who claimed to be of that lineage.

[†] The origin of the name Tancred is not explained in the novel. A hint of it appears in the description of an ancestor of the family, "one of the most distinguished knights in the third crusade, having saved the life of Coeur de Lion at the siege of Ascalon."[26] The historic Tancred, however, was a knight not in the third crusade but in the first. It was under the name of Tancred that the young Theodor Herzl (the founder of Zionism) had been inducted, as a student in Vienna, into a German nationalist fraternity after the ritual of a saber duel. Herzl later proposed that dueling be officially accredited in the state of Israel as a token of the aristocratic and nationalist spirit of the new country.

Sidonia, "divided between infidelity on one side and an anarchy of creeds on the other; with none competent to guide me, yet feeling that I must believe, for I hold that duty cannot exist without faith." Was it so unreasonable, he asks, to do what his ancestors would have done six centuries earlier? Sidonia listens to him sympathetically and replies, "It appears to me, Lord Montacute, that what you want is to penetrate the great Asian mystery."[28]

From London to Jerusalem—it is not only another world but another time-order that Tancred enters.* To penetrate the mystery of the East was to understand its history, which was an integral part of the present. The richness of that history becomes evident to him as he wanders from the garden of Gethsemane toward Bethany.

> Before him is a living, a yet breathing and existing city, which Assyrian monarchs came down to besiege, which the chariots of Pharaohs encompassed, which Roman Emperors have personally assailed, for which Saladin and Coeur de Lion, the Desert and Christendom, Asia and Europe, struggled in rival chivalry; a city which Mahomet sighed to rule, and over which the Creator alike of Assyrian kings and Egyptian Pharaohs and Roman Caesars, the Framer alike of the Desert and of Christendom, poured forth the full effusion of his divinely human sorrow.[30]

---

* Disraeli himself had made that voyage from London to Jerusalem in 1831, where he felt himself among "that sacred and romantic people from whom I derive by blood and name." Two years later the Jewish hero of another of his novels, *The Wondrous Tale of Alroy*, discovers, in the "Land of Promise," "all we have yearned after, all we have fought for, our beauteous country, our holy creed, our simple manners, and our ancient customs."[29]

Fatigued by his walk and lulled by the sound of the fountain, Tancred falls asleep and awakens to find a young woman standing before him, richly garbed and bejeweled, her face "the perfection of oriental beauty." Their conversation quickly establishes the fact that he is Christian and she Jewish, which prompts them to reflect upon the similarities and differences of their religions. The woman concludes that they have one thing in common: "We agree that half Christendom worships a Jewess, and the other half a Jew. . . . Which do you think should be the superior race, the worshipped or the worshipper?"[31] Tancred is about to answer, but she has vanished. She is later identified as Eva Besso, the "Rose of Sharon," the daughter of the Jewish banker to whom Sidonia had written a letter of introduction on behalf of Tancred.

Much of the novel is an adventure tale in an exotic setting, differing from that genre only because the characters are so intellectual and articulate. The adventures are brought about by Eva's foster-brother, Fakredeen, an unscrupulous and clever Syrian who is plotting to bring all of Palestine under his control. In the course of the Syrian's intrigues, Tancred is taken prisoner, wounded, and finally released, all the while engaging with his captor in animated discourses about their respective faiths. At one point, Tancred confesses his disappointment not with the physical constraints in which he finds himself but with his own spiritual condition. His presence in the Holy Land, he had thought, would bring him a sense of communion with the Holy Spirit. "But since I have been a dweller within its borders, and poured forth my passionate prayers at all its holy places, and received no sign, the desolating thought has sometimes come over my spirit, that there is a qualification of blood as well as of locality necessary for this communion, and that the favored votary must not only kneel in the Hold Land but be of the holy race."[32] Was he, he worries, not of that blood, an unwelcome visitor to this land? Was it only a morbid curiosity or aristocratic restlessness that had brought him here? He reassures himself. He has every right to be there, because it is the Creator, his Creator, that sanctified that land. He is not like the Indian Brahmin visiting Europe out of curiosity, a Europe that has no relation to him. The Holy Land has the most intimate relation to him, as a Briton.

> Vast as the obligations of the whole human family are to the Hebrew race, there is no portion of the modern populations so much indebted to them as the British people. . . . We are indebted to the Hebrew people for our knowledge of the true God and for the redemption from our sins. . . . I am not a traveling dilettante, mourning over a ruin, or in ecstasies at a deciphered inscription. I come to the land whose laws I obey, whose religion I profess, and I seek, upon its sacred soil, those sanctions which for ages were abundantly accorded.[33]

In the final scene of the book, in the garden of Bethany where they had first met, Eva expresses some of the doubts Tancred had earlier voiced. Had their heroic aspirations been dissipated, had they been dreaming about an unattainable end? "Your feelings," she tells him, "cannot be what they were before all this happened; when you thought only of a divine cause, of stars, of angels, and of our peculiar and gifted land. No, no; now it is all mixed up with intrigue, and politics, and management, and baffled schemes, and cunning arts of men. You may be, you are, free from all this, but your faith is not the same. You no longer believe in Arabia."* "Why, thou to me art Arabia," he insists. "Talk not to me of leaving a divine cause; why, thou

---

* "Arabia" meant Palestine, and "Arab" was equivalent to "Semite," meaning Jews as well as Arabs.

art my cause, and thou art most divine." She persists. "There are those to whom I belong, and to whom you belong. . . . Fly, fly from me, son of Europe and of Christ!" Why should he fly, he protests? He is a Christian in the land of Christ. He will not leave until she agrees that "our united destinies shall advance the sovereign purpose of our lives." If only she declares her love for him, he will sever the "world-worn bonds" that constrain them. That she cannot do. Her head falls upon his shoulder, he embraces her, but her cheek is cold, her hand lifeless. He sprinkles her with water from the fountain, she opens her eyes, sighs, and looks about her in bewilderment. At that moment noises are heard, people come trampling toward them, there are shouts calling for Lord Montacute, and the party appears. "The Duke and Duchess of Bellamont had arrived at Jerusalem."[34]

That memorable last sentence of the book comes as a shock to the reader. What are the Duke and Duchess doing in Jerusalem, and what does their arrival signify for Tancred and his "divine cause"? For that matter, what exactly is his cause? Does the arrival of the Duke and Duchess mean that that the established order is reasserting itself, fettering Tancred yet again with those "world-worn bonds"? Or does their presence in Jerusalem mean that they finally understand and sympathize with their son's aspirations? Most critics find fault not only with the denouement but with much of the latter part of the book, for Tancred never makes it clear what that "divine cause," the "new crusade," is. Disraeli, one might suspect, had simply given up toward the end, unable to resolve the problem he himself had raised.

Disraeli himself had no such doubts, no second thoughts about the spirit or intent of the novel. Some of the more audacious sentiments in it, uttered by Sidonia and Eva, were voiced by Disraeli himself in Parliament later that year, when he insisted that Jews, professing a "true religion," were the "authors" of Christianity.[35] He stopped short of saying then, what he did in *Tancred*, that "Christianity is Judaism for the multitude, but still it is Judaism."[36] Thirty years later, as Prime Minister much involved with the "Eastern question," he told his friend Benjamin Jowett, the Greek scholar and Master of Balliol, that *Tancred* was the favorite of his novels.[37]

If there is a problem about the meaning of *Tancred*, the solution may be found in another book by Disraeli, not a novel, written four years later. In the midst of his biography of George Bentinck (his friend and ally in the protectionist faction of the Tory Party), Disraeli inserted a quite gratuitous chapter, which does not even mention Bentinck, entitled "The Jewish Question." That chapter, an essay really, is nothing less than a paean to the Jewish "race" which, "sustained by a sublime religion," survived the hatred and persecution of centuries and produced gifted Jews in every sphere of life: "No existing race is so much entitled to the esteem and gratitude of society as the Hebrews." So far from being guilty of the crucifixion, they could proudly claim Jesus, "born from the chosen house of the chosen people," as one of them. Indeed, Jesus, the chapter concludes, is "the eternal glory of the Jewish race."[38] It is only in the next chapter that Disraeli explains that the views espoused in the earlier one were not, in fact, those of Bentinck, who had supported the bills admitting Jews to Parliament solely on the principle of religious liberty.*[39]

They were, however, very much the views of Disraeli—and of Tancred. This was the "great Asian mystery" revealed to

---

* Bentinck voted for those bills simply out of personal loyalty to Disraeli. "This Jewish question," he wrote to a friend in 1847, "is a terrible annoyance. . . . For my part, I don't think it matters two straws whether they are in or out of Parliament."[39]

Tancred in the "holy land" of that "holy race"—the eternal, transcendent quality of Judaism even in the age of Christianity. And this was the "new crusade" to which Tancred had dedicated himself, a crusade not by Christians against Muslims but by a Christian and a Jew united in a "sovereign purpose." Eva, the Jewess, may have faltered in the end, but Tancred, the Christian, did not. Nor did Disraeli, who embodied in himself the Jew and the Christian and who was steadfast to the end—a politician/novelist who was also the quintessential philosemite.

Daniel Deronda

George Eliot read *Tancred* shortly after its publication. It was "very thin," she complained, much inferior to *Coningsby* and *Sybil*.* She disapproved of Disraeli's Young Englandism but even more of his theory of race. So far from the purity of races being a condition of their superiority, it was a cause of their degeneration and, ultimately, of their extinction.

> The fellowship of race, to which D'Israeli [sic] so exultingly refers the munificence of Sidonia, is so evidently an inferior impulse which must ultimately be superseded that I wonder even he, Jew as he is, dares to boast of it. My Gentile nature kicks most resolutely against any assumption of superiority in the Jews, and is almost ready to echo Voltaire's vituperation. I bow to the supremacy of Hebrew poetry, but much of their early mythology and almost all their history is utterly revolting. Their stock has produced a Moses and a Jesus, but Moses was impregnated with Egyptian philosophy and Jesus

---

* Disraeli did not, however, read *Daniel Deronda* (or perhaps any other of Eliot's novels). Asked whether he had done so, he delivered the famous quip, "When I want to read a novel, I write one."[40]

---

is venerated and adored by us only for that wherein He transcended or resisted Judaism. The very exaltation of their idea of a national deity into a spiritual monotheism seems to have been borrowed from the other oriental tribes. Everything *specifically* Jewish is of a low grade.[41]

That was in 1848. In 1876, Eliot was to produce a novel that was almost as "exultingly" in favor of that "fellowship of race" as Sidonia himself.* Her novel differs from Disraeli's in one crucial respect. Tancred's crusade is cast in a universalist mode, a united Christianity and Judaism sharing a common purpose. Eliot and her hero Daniel Deronda have no such illusions. It is a national, not universal, sovereignty they seek for the Jews in Palestine, a "separate" nation that would incorporate universal ideals, to be sure, but that would be embodied in a distinctively Jewish state.

Like Deronda, Eliot had to undergo an initiation into Judaism. Born into a low-church Anglican family, inspired in her youth by an Evangelical teacher, and then converted to an agnosticism bordering on atheism by English Positivists and German Young Hegelians, she came to an appreciation of Judaism relatively late in life. She had already produced translations of such notable iconoclasts as David Strauss, Ludwig Feuerbach, and Baruch Spinoza, when she met, in 1866, a young Jewish emigré, Emanuel Deutsch, who inspired her to rethink all of her old views. Encouraged to learn Hebrew, she read some of the ancient and medieval classics of Judaism, as well as modern

---

* Eliot had also become better disposed to Disraeli as a politician. She was pleased when he triumphed over Gladstone in the election of 1874 and praised him both for his speeches in Parliament and for his handling of the "Russian question" at the Congress of Berlin in 1878. Defending his politics to a friend who thought him "unprincipled," she also recommended his novels as "wonderfully clever."[42]

commentaries. That extraordinary process of self-education and reevaluation was reflected, ten years later, in *Daniel Deronda*.*

As Eliot was initiated into Judaism by Deutsch, so her hero is by Mordecai, a clerk in a Jewish bookstore where Daniel happens to be browsing. Asked whether he is Jewish, Daniel tells him he is not. Yet Mordecai senses him to be one "of our race." Sickly and contemplating his death, Mordecai comes to see in Daniel a disciple who will carry on his vision of Judaism and his aspirations for the Jewish people. He himself, he explains, came to that vision not in England, where he was born, but while studying abroad where he was exposed to both Jewish and Christian culture.

> Then ideas, beloved ideas, came to me because I was a Jew.
> They were a trust to fulfil, because I was a Jew. They were
> an inspiration, because I was a Jew, and felt the heart of my
> race beating within me. They were my life; I was not fully
> born till then. . . . They [the medieval sages] had absorbed
> the philosophy of the Gentile into the faith of the Jew, and
> they still yearned toward a centre for our race. One of their

---

* Evidence of that education appears in the novel itself. The epigraph of one of the chapters is a passage from the German historian Leopold Zunz, the founder of Die Wissenschaft des Judentums ("the science of Judaism").

> If there are ranks in suffering, Israel takes precedence of all the nations—if the duration of sorrows and patience with which they are born ennoble, the Jews are among the aristocracy of every land—if a literature is called rich in the possession of a few classic tragedies, what shall we say to a National Tragedy lasting for fifteen hundred years, in which the poets and the actors were also the heroes?

This excerpt appears in German in the epigraph and is translated into English in the opening paragraph of the chapter, where Eliot explains that Deronda "had lately been reading that passage."[43] Deronda could have read it (although Eliot does not say so) in an English translation recently published. But Eliot herself had read it in the original, in Zunz's *Die Synagogale Poesie des Mittelalters*, and it is her translation that appears in the novel.

souls was born again within me, and awaked amid the memories of their world. It travelled into Spain and Provence; it debated with Aben-Ezra; it took ship with Jehuda ha-Levi; it heard the roar of the Crusaders and the shrieks of tortured Israel.[44]

It is that soul Mordecai wants to bequeath to Daniel. Daniel is moved by his tale but reminds him again that he is not Jewish. He had never known his parents and lives with his guardian, Sir Hugo, whom he believes to be his father. Undeterred by this report, Mordecai takes Daniel under his wing, introducing him to a discussion club of his friends, Jews and non-Jews, who are debating the momentous subject of "the law of progress." Against a self-described "rational Jew" who sees the assimilation of Jews as the natural course of progress, Mordecai propounds the opposite view, that the future of Judaism lies in the "separateness" and "unity of Israel," in Judaism as a "nationality" with "a land and a polity."

Looking towards a land and a polity, our dispersed people in all the ends of the earth may share the dignity of a national life which has a voice among the peoples of the East and the West. . . . I say that the effect of our separateness will not be completed and have its highest transformation unless our race takes on again the character of a nationality. . . . There is a store of wisdom among us to found a new Jewish polity, grand, simple, just, like the old—a republic where there is equality of protection. . . . Then our race shall have an organic center, a heart and brain to watch and guide and execute; the outraged Jew shall have a defence in the court of nations, as the outraged Englishman or American. And the world will gain as Israel gains. For there will be a community in the van of the East which carries the culture and the sympathies of every great nation in its bosom.[45]

The meeting with Mordecai, although central to its theme, comes relatively late in the novel. Before that Daniel had a more dramatic encounter under very different circumstances. He was rowing in the Thames when he observed a young woman who is about to throw herself into the river. He rescues her and hears her sad tale. Mirah is a Jewess born in England, brought up by her father, a wandering actor in Europe. She has come to England to find her mother and brother, about whom she knows nothing except that their name is Cohen, and she is in despair because her search has been in vain. Daniel befriends her and installs her in the home of a friend. As he learns more about her, he discovers that Mordecai is her long-lost brother.

The mystery of that relationship solved, so is the mystery of his own parentage, when his guardian, Sir Hugo, tells him that his mother, who has so far insisted upon anonymity, is dying and wants to meet her son. The meeting of mother and son in Genoa is as dramatic as the discipleship scene with Mordecai. Daniel now discovers that Mordecai is right; he is Jewish. But while Mordecai wants to instill in Daniel the soul of the Jewish sages, his mother has sought exactly the opposite, to free him from the burden, as she sees it, of that legacy. She herself, she tells him, wanted to be liberated from the double bondage of being a woman and a Jew. After her husband's death, to free herself in order to pursue her career as a singer and actress, and also to free her child from the onerous life of a Jew, she gave up her two-year-old son to her old friend and admirer, Sir Hugo, who promised to raise him as "an English gentleman."

Pleased to know that he is Jewish, Daniel rebukes her for having concealed his birthright. She justifies herself: "The bondage I hated for myself I wanted to keep you from. What better could the most loving mother have done? I relieved you from the bondage of having been born a Jew." The Judaism her father, an observant Jew, wanted to impose upon her was onerous because it was irrational as well as restrictive.

> I was to feel awe for the bit of parchment in the *mezuza* over the door; to dread lest a bit of butter should touch a bit of meat; to think it beautiful that men should bind the *tephillin* on them, and women not,—to adore the wisdom of such laws, however silly they might seem to me. . . . I was to care for ever about what Israel had been; and I did not care at all. I cared for the wide world, and all that I could represent in it. . . . You are glad to have been born a Jew. You say so. That is because you have not been brought up as a Jew. That separateness seems sweet to you because I saved you from it. [46]

A second meeting finds his mother in a more tender but still unrepentant mood. Would Deronda become the kind of Jew her father was, she wants to know? No, he assures her, his education and "Christian sympathies" will prevent that, but he will identify himself with his people and do what he can for them. She sees the irony of this turn of events. In spite of herself, she has been the instrument of her father's will; she has given him a grandson with "a true Jewish heart." "Every Jew," she quotes her father, "should rear his family as if he hoped that a Deliverer might spring from it." Hearing the echo of Mordecai in that sentiment, Daniel asks whether these were his exact words. Yes, he had actually written them. As for her, she hopes her son can forgive her, and if he wants to say *kaddish* for her, he should do so: "You will come between me and the dead." Almost as an afterthought, she asks whether Deronda is in love with a Jewess and whether that is why he is glad to be a Jew (not for that reason alone, he tells her), whether she is beautiful (yes), and whether she is ambitious to have "a path of her own" (no, that is not her nature).[47] Disappointed with the last answer, she nevertheless gives Deronda a jeweled miniature of her picture to be given to this woman who is so unlike herself.

Daniel is indeed in love with Mirah—and not with another woman who plays a large part in the book and whom his mother (as well as many of his readers and critics) would have preferred as his mate. Gwendolen, like his mother, aspires to be a liberated woman and is entirely focused on her own interests and desires. Her life takes a tragic turn when her husband, whom she married to escape from a life of poverty, turns out to be malevolent and despotic. Released from his tyranny when he is accidentally drowned, she is painfully conscious that she married him knowing that he had a long-time mistress and two illegitimate children, and, worse, that she could have saved him from drowning and made no effort to do so.

During much of this time, before and during her marriage, Gwendolen has sought Daniel's advice and comfort, looking upon him as a father-confessor and, as she sees it, an unrequited lover. Daniel, however, has other plans: to marry Mirah and with her carry out the mission bequeathed him by Mordecai.

> I am going to the East to become better acquainted with the condition of my race in various countries there. . . . The idea that I am possessed with is that of restoring a political existence to my people, making them a nation again, giving them a national centre, such as the English have, though they too are scattered over the face of the globe. That is a task

which presents itself to me as a duty: I am resolved to begin it, however feebly. I am resolved to devote my life to it. At the least, I may awaken a movement in other minds, such as has been awakened in my own.[48]

Gwendolen versus Mirah, Rebecca versus Rowena—critics would like to rewrite the novels and re-pair the couples. Just as Rebecca seems a more fitting and interesting mate for Ivanhoe, so Gwendolen is for Daniel. Indeed, both novels have been rewritten for just that purpose. In *Rebecca and Rowena*, Thackeray has Ivanhoe marrying Rebecca; in *Gwendolen Harleth*, F. R. Leavis, the literary critic, has Daniel marrying Gwendolen. These alternative novels are travesties, because neither takes the Jewish theme seriously. Rebecca will not marry out of her faith or be converted to Christianity; nor will Ivanhoe, the noted Saxon and champion of King Richard, be converted to Judaism. So too, Daniel, having assumed the mantle of Mordecai, can hardly leave the "true Jewess" Mirah in favor of Gwendolen, who is not Jewish, has no interest in Judaism, and can hardly help him in his mission to Palestine.

Leavis's rewriting of the novel went beyond the marital rearrangement. He also eliminated most of the Jewish theme—the "bad half" of the novel, as he put it—leaving only the Gwendolen story.* Other critics, Henry James, most notably, shared his distaste for that part of the novel, not because they were antisemitic (neither James nor Leavis was), but because they could not take seriously Daniel's (or Eliot's) view of Judaism and the

---

* Leavis's novel was never published, not because he had second thoughts about it, but because his publisher did. His proposed title page was:
GWENDOLEN HARLETH
George Eliot's superb last novel
liberated from
DANIEL DERONDA[49]

Jewish people. Eliot had anticipated that the "Jewish element" in the novel would "satisfy nobody."[50] What she could not have anticipated was the different form that criticism would take today by "Orientalists" like Edward Said, who object not only to the Zionist agenda proposed by Daniel, but to the "ethnocentric," "colonialist," and "imperialist hegemony" they see in it.[51]

Yet the book had admirers in Eliot's day and sold almost as well as her previous novel, *Middlemarch*. It was soon translated into German, French, and Russian, as well as Hebrew and Yiddish. And it still occupies a place in the "Great Tradition" of the novel—even in Leavis's classic account of that tradition, where George Eliot has the place of honor and *Daniel Deronda* is treated respectfully, although with serious reservations about the "bad half."[52] In retrospect, there is much to marvel at in the novel, in the "bad half" as well as the good. It is remarkable that Eliot, a Christian woman, should have written so movingly about Jews and Judaism, and so presciently about Palestine, not merely as a "homeland" but also as a "Jewish polity." (And so presciently about feminism as well, in the person of Daniel's mother.) Even more remarkable was her rationale for what was to be known as Zionism. Unlike Evangelicals who looked forward to the "restoration" of the Jews in the holy land as the precondition for the Second Coming of Christ, or later Zionists who sought in Palestine a refuge from antisemitism and persecution, Eliot rested her case on Judaism itself—the "soul" that had traveled throughout the ages and throughout the world and would finally come to rest in the land of its forefathers.

It is this vision of Judaism, as a people and a nation, that later appealed to many Jews, and not only Zionists, who said that *Daniel Deronda* had inspired them to rethink and reexperience their own lives and views. The English writer Israel Zangwill reported meeting a colonel commanding a Welsh regiment who said, "I am Daniel Deronda"; born a Christian of baptized

Jewish parents, he explained, the book had brought him back to his faith and his people.[53] Perhaps more surprising is the testimonial of Rabbi Zvi Yehuda Kook, the leader of the religious Zionist sect, who praised Eliot as one of the few Christians who understood the religious roots of Zionism.[54]

Another odd tribute comes from Lionel Trilling, whose essay "The Changing Myth of the Jew" concludes with *Daniel Deronda*, the most satisfactory of the "counter-myths," not only for Jews but for Gentiles as well who respond to "a genuine, inner, intimate quality" in the Jewish characters, a sense of "reality" and "credibility." "It does not too much strain the imagination, Trilling observes, to say 'Jews are like that'"; at least some Jews are like that, and to some degree. The final sentences of the essay remind the reader that in this novel, as in all novels, one must disentangle "the mythical from the actual"—a difficult task, "for in the mythical there is usually, of course, a little of what is true."[55]

Eliot herself took on that task of disentangling the mythical and the actual, finding in the mythical (in her novel) more than a little of the truth. Just as Disraeli reaffirmed the moral of *Tancred* in his speech in Parliament, so Eliot did the same for *Daniel Deronda* in an essay written two years later. *Daniel Deronda* was her last novel; *Impressions of Theophrastus Such* her last book; and "The Modern Hep! Hep! Hep!" the last and longest essay in that book.* She started writing it in June 1878,

---

* Eliot explained neither the title of the book nor that of the essay. She may have thought it insulting to her readers to identity Theophrastus, Aristotle's successor in the Peripatetic School. The expression "Hep! Hep! Hep!" appears in *Daniel Deronda* where Daniel, wandering in the Jewish neighborhood of London, is imagined transported back to the Rhineland at the end of the eleventh century, when "the Hep! Hep! Hep! of the Crusaders came like the bay of bloodhounds" and the missionaries fell upon the Jews with "sword and firebrand."[56] More recently (Eliot did not mention this but she must have had it in mind), "Hep! Hep!" had been the rallying cry of anti-Semitic rioters in Germany in 1819.

completed it in November, and had the satisfaction of reading it to her husband (as she thought of him), George Lewes, on his death-bed. It was published in May the following year, a few months after his death.

The essay puts the case for Jewish "separateness," or nationality, in spiritual as well as political terms: "The eminence, the nobleness of a people depends on its capability of being stirred by memories, and of striving for what we call spiritual ends—ends which consist not in immediate material possession, but in the satisfaction of a great feeling that animates the collective body as with one soul." It is not only the collective soul that is ennobled; it is also the soul of each citizen who is related to something larger than himself, "something great, admirable, pregnant with high possibilities, worthy of sacrifice." For Jews that sense of "separateness" is unique in its intensity because it is rooted in both revelation and history, and the dispersion of the people makes that history even more "exceptional." Tortured and exiled, a people of weaker nature might have given way to pressure and merged with the population around them. Instead, tenaciously holding on to their inheritance of blood and faith, they cherish all the more the differences that mark them off from their oppressors: "The separateness which was made their badge of ignominy would be their inward pride, their source of fortifying defiance." That separateness, to be sure, could also give rise to "answering vices" resulting from the abuses to which they are subject. But even the vices might be virtues, the condition of their survival. The virtues for which Jews are notable—the care for orphans and widows, women and children, family and community—withstood centuries of persecution and oppression because they are deeply ingrained in the Jewish religion and race.[57]

Nationality, then, is of the essence of Judaism. The question is whether there are enough worthy Jews, "some new

Ezras, some modern Maccabees," who by their heroic example would set about making their people "once more one among the nations."

> Every Jew should be conscious that he is one of a multitude possessing common objects of piety in the immortal achievements and immortal sorrows of ancestors who have transmitted to them a physical and mental type strong enough, eminent enough in faculties, pregnant enough with peculiar promise, to constitute a new beneficent individuality among the nations, and, by confuting the traditions of scorn, nobly avenge the wrongs done to their Fathers.[58]

This might have been Deronda or Mordecai speaking. It was Eliot in her last testament. She died a year and a half later.

Literary philosemitism had come a long way in the course of the century. And so had literary antisemitism—in reverse. By 1876, when *Daniel Deronda* was published, blatantly antisemitic novels were no longer respectable. Dickens's Fagin had appeared in 1838. Dickens, it was said at the time, was a "low writer"; he wrote about low subjects for a low audience.[59*] Fagin was perhaps the lowest of his characters, a criminal and corrupter of children as well as an exploiter of the poor. A quarter of a century later, Eliza Davis, a Jewish woman (the wife of the solicitor who had bought his home), accused Dickens of encouraging, in the figure of Fagin, "a vile prejudice against the

---

* Queen Victoria, reading the book over the objections of her mother (who disapproved of "light" as well as "low" books), found *Oliver Twist* "excessively interesting" and recommended it to her Prime Minister, Lord Melbourne. He confessed he could not get beyond the first chapters. "It's all among Workhouses, and Coffin Makers, and Pickpockets. I shouldn't think it would tend to raise morals; I don't like that low debasing view of mankind. . . . I don't like them in reality, and therefore I don't wish them represented."[60]

despised Hebrew" and appealed to him to "atone for a great wrong on a whole though scattered nation." Dickens protested that that was not at all his intention. In the period portrayed in the novel, it was unfortunately true that "that class of criminal almost invariably *was* a Jew"; moreover, the other wicked characters in the novel were Christian.[61] In the next edition of *Oliver Twist*, Dickens softened, ever so slightly, the image of Fagin by referring to him by name instead of as "the Jew," thus making "the Jew" less of an epithet and making Fagin less conspicuously, or at least specifically, Jewish. He performed a more serious act of atonement in 1864 in *Our Mutual Friend*, his last completed novel, which features Riah, an "old Jewish man," a "gentle Jew," an altogether admirable character, in contrast to Fledgeby, his "Christian master," "the meanest cur existing."[62] Mrs. Davis thanked him for "a great compliment paid to myself and to my people," and was particularly taken with the "very picturesque" character of Riah.[63*]

Dickens's Jews, for good or bad, were of the lower classes. Anthony Trollope's were unmistakeably upper-class. A staunch Liberal, Trollope had a special animus against Jews because of his intense dislike for Disraeli, who was not only a Jew (by birth at least) but a Tory, and, worse yet, a novelist who received larger advances for his novels than Trollope did for his. A money-lender in *Barchester Towers* (1857) was called Sidonia after Disraeli's character, and an especially unprincipled Tory politician in *Phineas Finn* (1869) was clearly patterned on Disraeli himself. Yet that later novel also featured Madame Goesler, the daughter of a German Jewish attorney and widow of a Jewish banker, who is one of the most intelligent and high-minded of Trollope's characters. One critic described her as "the most

---

* A more caustic comment was Lionel Trilling's, who found Riah "as impossibly good as Fagin was impossibly bad."[64]

perfect gentleman" in his novels—than which, for Trollope, there could be no higher praise (although he would surely have demurred at calling a lady a "gentleman").[65]

Like Dickens, Trollope was more repentant in his later years. *The Way We Live Now*, in 1875, the most bitter of his novels, exposed the mercenary values of the new commercial society, which afflicted most of the characters and all aspects of life including love and marriage. Among its many villains, the worst was the dishonest speculator Augustus Melmotte, who was ambiguously Jewish, assumed to be so because his wife was vaguely East European. Melmotte's disreputable associate, Cohenlupe, was unmistakeably Jewish. On the other hand, Eze-kiel Brehgert, who "went to a synagogue on a Saturday" and was "absolutely a Jew," was an honest banker, decent, intel-ligent, and thoroughly honorable. He proposed marriage to a "Christian lady" who accepted him for the most materialistic reasons, and then withdrew his proposal because he could not provide the magnificent house she had made a condition of mar-riage. "I behaved like a gentleman," he explained—a view evi-dently shared by the author.[66]

By the third quarter of the century, the familiar kind of liter-ary antisemitism was much abated. The stereotypes and preju-dices remained, in society and in the culture, but they were less virulent and less intrusive. As the political aspect of the Jewish question was amicably resolved, so, too, the cultural and social aspects were, not resolved, to be sure, but much alleviated. When *Daniel Deronda* was published, the year after *The Way We Live Now*, the reader would not be surprised to encounter a Jewish hero who was also, as his mother said, an "English gentleman." What was surprising, and what made the book so controversial, was not so much the philosemitism that accompanied this social acceptance as the philo-Zionism that seemed to flow from the philosemitism. It was not only individual Jews who were judged and accepted as individuals, in society as in the polity, but Jews as a "separate" people deemed worthy of their own homeland in the place of their historic origin—all this before either "philosemitism" or "Zionism" entered the vocabulary.

A footnote to this Victorian saga brings it into the following century with a notable example of literary antisemitism transmuted into philosemitism. The most quoted passage in John Buchan's most popular novel, *The Thirty-Nine Steps* (written early in World War I), describes Jewish anarchists conspiring with Jewish capitalists to bring Russia and Germany to a war that would involve Britain and devastate all of Europe.

> "For three hundred years they [the Jews] have been persecuted, and this is the return match for pogroms. The Jew is everywhere, but you have to go far down the backstairs to find him. . . . But if you're on the biggest kind of job and are bound to get to the real boss, ten to one you are brought up against a little white-faced Jew in a bath-chair with an eye like a rattlesnake. Yes, sir, he is the man who is ruling the world just now . . ."[67]

This portrait of the villain appears on the fifth page of the novel and haunts much of the rest of it. The hero and narrator, Richard Hannay, looking out for that rattlesnaked-eye Jew and his accomplices, tries to outwit them in a series of breathtaking adventures. But the passage is deceptive, for it is not Richard Hannay, who describes that Jew so vividly. It is a Mr. Scudder, an American (from Kentucky), who warns Hannay of that nefarious character and his conspiracy. And it is Hannay who soon discovers that the whole story is "a pack of lies."[68] There is a conspiracy, to be sure, but it is led by German spies, not by Jewish anarchists or capitalists. For the rest of the book,

Germans are the villains while Jews disappear from the scene. Even the word is absent, except for the explanation that Scudder "had a lot of odd biases. . . . Jews, for example, made him see red. Jews and the high finance."[69]

This is not to acquit Buchan of the charge of antisemitism. There are Jewish capitalists and financiers, communists and anarchists, in his novels, along with the familiar antisemitic and pejorative gibes. But there are also non-Jewish capitalists and financiers who are villainous, and Jewish capitalists and financiers who are honorable, even heroic. Hannay himself (who features in other of Buchan's novels) is something of a capitalist—a South African mining engineer who boasts of having "got my pile—not one of the big ones, but good enough for me."[70*] Even the Jewish villains are not the nastiest of villains; in *Mr. Standfast* (1919), he is the most decent of the lot. *The Three Hostages* (1924), the last of the Hannay quintet, introduces Julius Victor, an American banker who had been financially helpful to Britain during the war, and who is "one of the richest men in the world" (a few pages later he is "the richest man in the world"). He is also, incidentally, a Jew. Hannay recalls being told by a friend "who didn't like his race," that he was "the whitest Jew since the apostle Paul."[72] In the novel he is a very white Jew, not the perpetrator but the victim of another conspiracy precisely because his mission is to secure peace in the world. Moreover, his beautiful daughter, a Jewess, is the fiancée of the Marquis de la Tour du Pin, one of Hannay's oldest and noblest friends, and, of course, a Christian.

---

* In one of Buchan's earliest tales, *A Lodge in the Wilderness* (1906), an American woman describes a Jewish financier: "I like his face; there is a fire somewhere behind his eyes. But then I differ from most of my countrymen in liking Jews. . . . They are never vulgar at heart. If we must have magnates, I would rather Jews had the money. It doesn't degrade them and they have the infallible good taste of the East at the back of their heads."[71]

He "didn't like his race"—this was the familiar, almost reflexive antisemitism of the time, in fiction as in reality. So long as the world itself was normal, this kind of antisemitism was disagreeable but not perilous. It was when the conspiracies of the adventure tales became the realities of German politics that Buchan, acutely sensitive to the precarious nature of civilization, realized that what was permissible under civilized conditions was not permissible with civilization *in extremis*. This atonement (if it can be called that) manifested itself in his personal life as well as his novels. As early as 1930, before most Englishmen had become conscious of the nature of Nazism, Buchan, as a Member of Parliament (and an acquaintance of Chaim Weizmann), took up the cause of Zionism. In an article, "Ourselves and the Jews," he defended the Balfour Declaration as "a categorical promise" binding upon the government. Two years later he was elected chairman of the Parliamentary Pro-Palestine (that is, pro-Zionist) Committee, and two years after that he spoke at a mass demonstration organized by the Jewish National Fund: "When I think of Zionism I think of it in the first place as a great act of justice. It is reparation for the centuries of cruelty and wrong which have stained the record of nearly every Gentile people."[73]

It may seem ironic that the man associated with the fictional Jewish-capitalist-communist conspiracy should have had his name inscribed, in solemn ceremony, in the Golden Book of the Jewish National Fund. Buchan himself would have found nothing ironic about this. His speech acknowledging this honor took as its theme the racial similarities of Scotsmen (like himself) and Jews, with particular reference to their high regard for learning. A participant in the ceremony, sharing the platform with Buchan, recalled his behavior during the address following his, when Buchan leaned forward and watched, with unconcealed delight and fascination, the ample gestures and bodily movements of a Yiddish-speaking rabbi.[74] One wonders what Buchan the novelist, the sometime antisemite, would have done with that scene.*

Buchan had come a long way from that memorable rattle-snaked-eye Jew in *The Thirty-Nine Steps*—as had the literary canon itself, the myths and counter-myths of fiction ranging from unabashed antisemitism to enthusiastic philosemitism. So too, philosemitism, in reality as well as in fiction, was to come a long way from the philo-Zionist sentiments of religious thinkers and preachers to the Zionist proclamations of politicians and statesmen.

---

* It is also intriguing to learn that the last books Buchan was reading shortly before his death in February 1940 (he was then Lord Tweedsmuir, the Governor General of Canada) were Lionel Trilling's *Matthew Arnold* and Werner Jaeger's *Paideia, The Ideals of Greek Culture.*[75]

V.

From Evangelicalism to Zionism

"An Evangelical among Evangelicals"

"Looking towards a land and a polity"—that was the animating spirit of Judaism according to George Eliot (by way of Mordecai and Deronda) in 1876, and in Eliot's own voice somewhat later.[1] Half a century earlier, British Evangelicals had initiated a movement for the "Restoration of Jews" to Palestine, primarily as a land rather than as a polity.* Like Eliot, they looked to Palestine not as a refuge from persecution but as a fulfillment of religious aspirations—millenarianism for themselves, the return to their "holy land" for the Jews.

Lord Ashley was one of the initiators and leaders of this movement—"an Evangelical of the Evangelicals," as he described himself.[2] Although a Tory Member of Parliament, he had the closest relations (literally, relations) with the reigning Whig aristocracy. His wife's stepfather (her biological father, it was rumored) was Lord Palmerston, and his mother-in-law was

---

* To the cynical ear today, the expression "Restoration of Jews" may have an antisemitic ring, suggesting a desire to rid England of undesirable Jews. There is no hint of that in the contemporary usage of the term.

the sister of Lord Melbourne. During the years when two of Ashley's objectives were carried out (a consulship and a bishopric in Jerusalem), his uncle was the Prime Minister and his wife's stepfather was the Foreign Secretary. He was also distinguished in his own right as a zealous social reformer and a no less zealous missionary to and for the Jews. In 1826, he noted in his diary: "Who will be the Cyrus of Modern Times, the second Chosen to restore the God's people?"[3] (Cyrus, the king of Persia, had issued a decree permitting the exiled Jews to return to Palestine.) A new member of Parliament, Ashley was all of twenty-five when he wrote that. A decade later he became a patron of the London Society for Promoting Christianity Amongst the Jews (the Jews' Society, as it was known), which counted among its founding members another notable Evangelical, William Wilberforce. The original agenda of the Society read:

Declaring the Messiahship of Jesus to the Jew first and also
to the non-Jew.
Endeavouring to teach the Church its Jewish roots.
Encouraging the physical restoration of the Jewish people to
Eretz Israel—the Land of Israel.
Encouraging the Hebrew Christian/Messianic Jewish
movement.[4]

The Society was not very successful in achieving its primary purpose, the conversion of the Jews; in its first thirty years it reported a total of only two-hundred-odd converts. But it undertook other missions on behalf of Jews, such as protests against the antisemitic decrees in Russia. By the time Ashley became active in it, much of its public focus was on the third item in its agenda, the Restoration of Jews—not merely to Palestine but to "Eretz Israel."

Because of his family connections, Ashley played a major role in encouraging Britain's involvement in Palestine. It was he who convinced Palmerston, in 1838, to include in a commercial treaty a provision for the appointment of a British consul to Jerusalem, one of whose functions was to protect the lives and property of Jewish settlers. It was a vice-consul, not a consul, who was appointed, but Britain was the first power to have a consul of any rank in Jerusalem. Ashley was exultant. For him (although not Palmerston) this was the first step in the ultimate goal, the Restoration of Jews.

> What a wonderful event it is! The ancient city of the people
> of God is about to resume a place among the nations, and
> England is the first of the Gentile Kingdoms that "ceases to
> trod her down". . . . I shall always remember that God put
> it into my heart to conceive the plan for His honor, gave me
> influence to prevail with Palmerston and provided a man for
> the situation, who can remake Jerusalem in his mirth.[5]

A few months later, reviewing a book on the Near East, Ashley spoke of the growing interest in Palestine on the part of Christians who revered the "Hebrew people" and respected their desire to return to the holy land. "We must learn to behold this nation with the eyes of reverence and affection; we must honor in them the remnant of a people which produced poets like Isaiah and Joel; kings like David and Josiah; and ministers like Joseph, Daniel and Nehemiah; but above all, as that chosen race of men, of whom the Savior of the world came according to the flesh."[6]

In 1840, emboldened by the success of the consulship and provoked by yet another episode in the perennial "Eastern Question," Ashley drew up a document to be presented to Palmerston making the case for the Restoration in practical terms that would appeal to the Foreign Secretary. At the moment, he pointed out, the vast area between the Euphrates and the Mediterranean was nearly desolate, its produce was minimal, and as a source of revenue it was almost worthless. To acquire the labor and capital required to revive the economy, immigrants and settlers had to be assured that life and property would be secure. To that end, he proposed that the European powers join with Syria to create an authority that would bring peace and order to the area. The ideal immigrants would be Jews, who had the required industrial virtues as well as the spiritual longing to return to the land of their fathers.

> There are many reasons why more is to be anticipated from them [the Jews] than from any others who might settle there. They have ancient reminscences and deep affection for the land; it is connected in their hearts with all that is bright in their past, and with all that is right in those which are to come; their industry and perseverance are prodigious; they subsist, and cheerfully, on the smallest pittance. . . . Long ages of suffering have trained their people to habits of endurance and self-denial; they would joyfully exhibit them in the settlement and service of their ancient country.[7]

There is no record of any official response to this document. Ashley himself had no illusions about Palmerston's enthusiasm for this or any other religious cause, which is why he appealed to Britain's interest in the security and stability of the area. Palmerston, Ashley wrote in his diary, was "chosen by God to be an instrument of good to His ancient people, to do homage as it were to their inheritance, and to recognize their rights"—"without," he added, "believing their destiny."[8] Lady Palmerston evidently shared her husband's indifference. To her friend, the widow of the Russian ambassador to Britain, she explained: "We [the Whigs] have on our side the fanatical and religious elements, and you know what a following they have in this country. They are absolutely determined that Jerusalem and the whole of Palestine shall be reserved for the Jews to return to—this is their only longing."[9]

Another event the following year brought Palestine again to the attention of Ashley. The initiative this time came from an unlikely source, the King of Prussia. Provoked by a treaty recognizing the sovereignty of Turkey in Palestine, the King proposed the creation in Jerusalem of a Protestant bishopric under the joint sponsorship of Anglicans and Lutherans. Ashley and the London Society enthusiastically took up the cause. Over the strong objections of Gladstone and other Anglicans, who disliked any association with Lutherans, Ashley prevailed upon the new Prime Minister, Robert Peel, to support the bill creating the bishopric. The first bishop to be appointed to that post was Michael Solomon Alexander, a converted Jew, the son of a rabbi and himself a former rabbi. Ashley, who had been involved in that choice, was delighted. He found it "overwhelming," as he confided to his diary, "to see a native Hebrew appointed by the Church of England to carry back to the Holy City the truths and blessings which Gentiles had received from it."[10]* A few days later, after attending the first sermon delivered by the bishop, he reported: "I can rejoice in Zion for a capital, in Jerusalem for a church, and in a Hebrew for a king."[11] For the rest of his life, Ashley wore the ring the bishop had given him before leaving for Jerusalem. It was inscribed with a quotation from the

---

* It was, indeed, a remarkable choice. Born to an English Jewish family living in Germany, Alexander emigrated to England in 1820, where he became the rabbi in Norwich and then a Hebrew teacher and *shochet* in Plymouth. In 1825 he converted to Christianity, moved to Dublin where he taught Hebrew, and was ordained a priest in the Anglican Church. He worked for the London Society, first in Danzig and then in London. He was a professor of Hebrew at King's College when he received the appointment as bishop in Jerusalem.

Psalms: "Oh, pray for the peace of Jerusalem; they shall prosper that love thee."[12]

The next crisis in the Near East was the occasion for yet another attempt by Lord Shaftesbury (as he then was) to pursue the cause of the Restoration of Jews. In 1853, on the eve of the Crimean War and again the following year, he urged Lord Clarendon, the Foreign Minister, to try to persuade Turkey to cede some land to the Jews. In his diary, again citing the decree of Cyrus, he argued that this was the time for an "analogous" action.

> All the East is stirred; the Turkish Empire is in rapid
> decay; every nation is restless; all hearts expect some great
> thing. . . . Syria "is wasted without an inhabitant"; these vast
> and fertile regions will soon be without a ruler, without a
> known and acknowledged power to obtain dominion. The
> territory must be assigned to some one or other; can it be
> given to any European potentate? to any American colony?
> to any Asiatic sovereign or tribe? . . . No, no, no! There is
> a country *without a nation*; and God now, in His wisdom
> and mercy, directs us to *a nation without a country*. His own
> once loved, nay, still loved people, the sons of Abraham, of
> Isaac, and of Jacob.[13]

Those phrases—"country without a nation" and "nation without a country"—have since become memorable, echoed in the famous Zionist slogan: "A land without a people for a people without a land." That slogan has become a subject of much controversy. Attributed by Edward Said to Israel Zangwill in 1901, it is the source of Said's charge that Zionists wilfully propagated the idea that there were no "people" in Palestine.[14] In fact, the phrase had been coined by an Evangelical clergyman in 1843, who was well aware that the country was populated because he had traveled there. By "people," he, like later Zionists, meant a unified people recognizable as a nation.

Shaftesbury's later interventions on this subject were more modest but in the same spirit. The Palestine Exploration Fund he helped establish in 1865 continued the focus on Palestine. By sending out agents to explore and survey every corner of the land, he explained in his presidential speech to the society, they were preparing it for "the return of its ancient possessors, for I must believe that the time cannot be far off before that great event will come to pass." Echoing his diary comments twenty years earlier, he observed that the land was "almost without an inhabitant—a country without a people, and look! Scattered over the world, a people without a country." He also recalled the inscribed ring that had been given him almost a quarter-and-a-century earlier, which he was still wearing that day.[15] The following year, in an article in the *Quarterly Review*, he appealed to a wider audience.

> The country wants capital and population. The Jew can give it both. And has not England a special interest in promoting such a restoration? . . . The nationality of the Jews exists; the spirit is there and has been for three thousand years, but the external form, the crowning bond of union, is still wanting. A nation must have a country. The old land, the old people. This is not an artificial experiment; it is nature, it is history.[16]

This is Shaftesbury, the most ardent of philosemites, respectful to Jews personally (he bowed to them when he passed them in Germany, to their astonishment), and reverential to them as a people and a nation—although not, as the parliamentary debates show, willing to admit them to Parliament. In other respects, as his contemporaries and biographers have testified, he was a difficult and troubled man, depressed, suspicious, temperamental, severely judgmental of himself and even more harshly of others. There was nothing saintly in the personal character of this most "Evangelical of the Evangelicals." But there was an abundance of good works to his credit, reflecting his genuine concern for the poor and his untiring efforts on their behalf. One biographer concludes that, for all his personal faults, he was "one of the greatest Victorians, and, in however curious a manner, one of the best."[17] So one might also say that he was, if not one of the greatest or best philosemitic Victorians—George Eliot might rival him for that title—surely one of the most exuberantly philosemitic ones.*

Jewish Zionism and English Philo-Zionism

As Evangelicalism began to ebb in late Victorian England, so did the rhetoric of philosemitism. So, too, the religious idea of the Restoration gave way to the political idea of Zionism. The organizational impetus for Zionism came not from Britain, where the idea had been anticipated by novelists as well as Evangelicals, and not from the Anglo-Jewish community, which had the prestige and resources to further the cause, but from Jews abroad. Apart from a few exceptions, among the Rothschilds and Montefiores in particular, most of the prominent and affluent English Jews were hostile to Zionism, fearful that a homeland in Palestine would make them "aliens" in their own country. European Jews had no such compunctions. Antisemi-

---

* There is no evidence of any relationship or even communication between Eliot and Shaftesbury. (Eliot died in 1892, Shaftesbury in 1895.) But they agreed in paying tribute to Disraeli. "D'Israeli," Shaftesbury wrote shortly after his death, "is a Hebrew, and that to my mind always imparts a certain sense of reverence. I can never forget that of this race our blessed Lord came according to his flesh."[18]

tism in Germany and East Europe, repeated pogroms in Russia, the Damascus Affair in 1840 (the accusation of ritual murder), and the Dreyfus Affair in 1894 (the accusation of treason) gave them a more urgent sense of danger within their own countries and a willingness to look elsewhere for security. It was an Austrian Jew, in 1890, who coined the word "Zionism" (and who may later have regretted it when he became the founder and leader of an anti-Zionist party).* And it was a Hungarian Jew, in 1896, who wrote, in German, the book that inspired the world-wide Zionist movement.

As the Paris correspondent for a Viennese paper, Theodor Herzl was in the courtroom when Dreyfus was pronounced guilty and witnessed the scene in the courtyard when the captain was stripped of his military insignia to the shouts of "Death to Dreyfus! Death to the Jews!" Herzl later said that it was the Dreyfus Affair that prompted him to write *Der Judenstaat*, declaring the establishment of a Jewish state in Palestine,"our ever-memorable historic homeland," the only solution to the Jewish question.[19] That pamphlet, published in 1896, became, in effect, the founding document of Zionism. He himself became the founding father of Zionism by organizing the Zionist Congress that met in Basel the following year.

In 1885, a ten-year old Chaim Weizmann, living in the pale in a small town in Russia and recalling the pogroms a few years earlier, wrote a letter to his teacher explaining why Jews had to return to Zion: "All have decided: the Jews must die, but England will nevertheless have mercy upon us."[20] The boy

---

* "Zionism" (derived from the Hebrew word *"tsiyon,"* hill—that is, Jerusalem) first appeared in a journal edited by Nathan Birnbaum, *Selbstemanzipation*. Birnbaum attended the first Zionist Congress in 1897, but later turned against the idea of political Zionism and became the first Secretary General of Agudath Israel, the religious anti-Zionist organization.

was remarkably prescient, for in spite of the fact that much of the leadership and rank-and-file of the Zionist movement came from abroad, England, even in these early years, played a prominent part in it. Extracts from *Der Judenstaat*, in English, appeared in the London *Jewish Chronicle* in January 1896, a month before the German book was published in Vienna. In 1900, Herzl, addressing the Zionist Congress meeting for the first time in London (the earlier meetings, like some of the later ones, were in Basel), explained that England was the only country where "God's old people" were not subject to antisemitism. "England, free and mighty England, whose vision embraces the seven seas, will understand us and our aspirations. It is here that the Zionist movement, we may be sure, will soar to further and greater heights."[21] Herzl died in 1904, the same year, as it happened, that Chaim Weizmann took up residence in Manchester as a professor of chemistry at the university. Six years later Weizmann became a British subject. Assuming the role of intermediary between English Jews and English statesmen, he became, in effect, Herzl's successor.

The outbreak of the war brought Palestine, and with it Zionism, to the attention of the British government. It also revived interest in Zionism among Jews themselves. Following the pogroms in Russia in 1903, the Zionist movement had been deflected by proposals for the establishment of a Jewish colony in East Africa, preferably Uganda. Seriously considered for a while by the Colonial Secretary, Joseph Chamberlain, it was firmly rejected by the Zionist Congress.* When Turkey entered the war on the side of the Central Powers, British forces invaded

---

* As late as December, 1914, Weizmann entertained the idea, facetiously, one assumes, of a colony in "something like Monaco, with a university instead of a gambling-hall."[22]

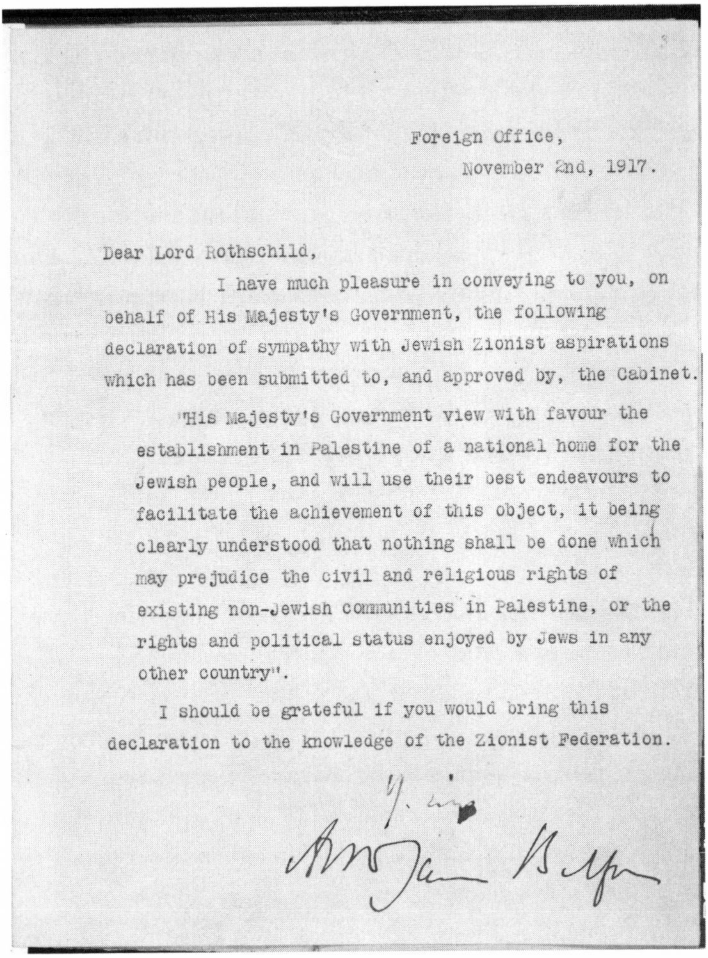

FIGURE 2 The Balfour Declaration © The British Library Board, Add. 41178, f.3

Palestine with the intention of detaching Palestine from the Turkish empire. This was the primary purpose of the Balfour Declaration issued by the coalition government headed by the Liberal Prime Minister David Lloyd George, with the Conservative Arthur Balfour as Foreign Secretary.

The Balfour Declaration was not a law enacted by Parliament. It was, literally, a "declaration" passed by the Cabinet on October 31, 1917. Moreover, it was not released directly to the public, but rather incorporated in a personal letter on Foreign Office stationery dated November 2, 1917, addressed to Lord Rothschild and signed by Arthur James Balfour. Opening with the explanation that the Cabinet had approved this "declaration of sympathy with Jewish Zionist aspirations," the letter went on to quote that declaration:

> His Majesty's government view with favor the establishment in Palestine of a national home for the Jewish people, and will use their best endeavors to facilitate the achievement of this object, it being clearly understood that nothing shall be done which may prejudice the civil and religious rights of existing non-Jewish communities in Palestine, or the rights and political status enjoyed by Jews in any other country.[23]

The letter concluded with the request that Lord Rothschild pass it on to the Jewish Federation. It reached the public a week later when it was published by the *Times*.

It was in this indirect fashion that the Declaration was issued. And it was in this ambiguous form that it became the center of Zionist aspirations and frustrations until the establishment of the state of Israel three decades later.[24] The ambiguities were deliberate. The phrase "national home"—"home," not "state"—fell short of the Zionist ideal; and "national" was qualified by the proviso recognizing the rights of "existing non-

Jewish communities in Palestine" and of "Jews in any other country." These were concessions to the opponents in the cabinet, of whom Edwin Montagu, one of two Jews in the cabinet, was the most vigorous. He was especially concerned lest the "rights and political status" of English Jews be prejudiced by the existence of a "national home" elsewhere. (The other Jew in the cabinet, Herbert Samuel, was a strong supporter of the Declaration.)* Within a week, a League of British Jews, consisting of some of the most prominent Jews, was founded for the purpose of opposing this and any other Zionist venture.

Balfour's motives, like those of Lloyd George, have been much debated. To what extent did they reflect the imperial ambitions of Britain, and to what extent a concern for Jews and Zionism? The answer is almost certainly both. Balfour's family background was very different from that of Lloyd George. His mother, a direct descendant of the Cecils, was a daughter of Lord Salisbury; his godfather was the Duke of Wellington; and his immediate predecessor as Prime Minister, in 1902, was his uncle, Salisbury. Yet his Scottish background did for him what Lloyd George's Welsh one did for him. Balfour's niece (and biographer) Blanche Dugdale reported that his life-long interest in Judaism originated in "the Old Testament training" he received from his mother and from the Scottish culture in which he was raised, and that his later studies in Jewish philosophy and literature contributed to the growing "intellectual admiration and sympathy" he felt for Jews and Judaism. She herself, as a child, imbibed from him the idea that "Christian religion and

---

* The religious make-up of the cabinet is interesting. Seven of the nine Christians were raised as Evangelicals or embraced Evangelicalism later in life; three were sons of the manse; one was a Scottish Methodist. There were no Catholics, two Jews, and only one Anglican. The ethnic composition is equally curious. Lloyd George was Welsh, Balfour and three others were Scottish or had lived in Scotland for long periods, one was an Irish Protestant, one was born in South Africa, and one in Germany.[25]

civilization owes to Judaism an immeasurable debt, shamefully ill repaid."[26] A visitor to the Balfour home in Scotland in 1895, when he was the Conservative leader in the House, recalled their after-dinner conversation about "the Jews, alien immigration, synagogues, chorus, churches," which ended with his reading a chapter from Isaiah "beautifully and reverently."[27] (He may have been stimulated on that occasion by the fact that his visitor, Lady Constance Battersea, was a Rothschild by birth.)

Politically, Balfour had not always been so well disposed to Jews. Like most in his party, he supported the Aliens Bill of 1905 restricting Jewish immigration. The following year, prompted by the Uganda scheme which he was inclined to favor, he arranged to meet Weizmann to ask why he was opposed to it. The Zionist movement, Weizmann told him, had a spiritual as well as a practical side, sustained by "a deep religious conviction expressed in modern political terms." Weizmann put the question to Balfour: "Supposing I were to offer you Paris instead of London, would you take it?" "But Dr. Weizmann," Balfour retorted, "we have London." "That is true," Weizmann said, "But we had Jerusalem when London was a suburb." Asked whether there were many Jews who thought like him, Weizmann assured him that there were millions. "If that is so," Balfour told him, "you will one day be a force."[28] They did not meet again until 1914, when they became good friends.

By the time the Declaration was passed, Balfour had a strong intellectual and moral as well as a political commitment to Zionism. Privately, he went further than the concept of a "home" for Jews, confessing that he himself looked forward to the time when Palestine would become a "Jewish state."[29] The introduction he wrote in 1919 to a book on Zionism by his friend Nahum Sokolow, a Polish writer living in England, was reprinted the following year in a volume of his own essays. It is surprisingly effusive, in contrast to the restrained, often skeptical, tone of most of his writings. Balfour recalled his early support for the Uganda project, which had many merits. "But it had one serious defect. It was not Zionism. It attempted to find a home for men of Jewish religion and Jewish race in a region far removed from the country where that race was nurtured and that religion came into being." Weizmann convinced him that that history could not be ignored, that the homeless people could find a home only in Palestine.

> The position of the Jews is unique. For them race, religion and country are inter-related, as they are inter-related in the case of no other race, no other religion, and no other country on earth. In no other case are the believers in one of the greatest religions of the world to be found (speaking broadly) only among the members of a single small people; in the case of no other religion is its past development so intimately bound up with the long political history of a petty territory wedged in between States more powerful far than it could ever be; in the case of no other religion are its aspirations and hopes expressed in language and imagery so utterly dependent for their meaning on the conviction that only from this one land, only through this one history, only by this one people, is full religious knowledge to spread through all the world.[30]

There were many Jews, Balfour knew (he personally knew them), who were hostile to Zionism because they felt that the very existence of a "homeland" would adversely affect their position in their "adopted" land. That was not so, he assured them. Prejudice, where it existed, did not originate with Zionism; nor did Zionism aggravate it. On the contrary, Jews everywhere could benefit by "assimilating" their status to that of all other people—that is, by acquiring what all other nations have, "a local habitation and a national home." Palestine would not solve the "Jewish question," but it would be of spiritual and material benefit to those Jews who could return to their homeland, as well as to those who could not or chose not to return. Zionism, he concluded, should be supported by "all men of good-will, whatever their country and whatever their creed."[31]

In the course of this warm defense of Zionism, Balfour defended the Jews against the popular and unfortunate image of them.

> The Jews have never been crushed. Neither cruelty nor contempt, neither unequal laws nor illegal oppression, have ever broken their spirit, or shattered their unconquerable hopes. But it may well be true that, where they have been compelled to live among their neighbors as if these were their enemies, they have obtained, and sometimes deserved, the reputation of being undesirable citizens. Nor is this surprising. If you oblige many men to be money-lenders, some will assuredly be usurers. If you treat an important section of the community as outcasts, they will hardly shine as patriots. Thus does intolerance blindly labor to create the justification for its own excesses.[32]

Three years later, in a debate in the House of Lords on a motion to reject the Mandate, Balfour had occasion to repeat these sentiments and vindicate the Jews from the prejudices held against them. He reminded his peers of the "absolutely unique" role the Jews play in the "intellectual, the artistic, the philosophic and scientific development of the world," to say nothing, he added ironically, of the "economic side of their energies," of which Christians were all too aware. "You will find them in every university, in every center of learning; and at the very moment when they were being persecuted . . . by the Church, their philosophers were developing thoughts which the great doctors of the Church embodied in their religious system." The purpose of the Mandate was to provide a home for this remarkable people, where they could cultivate, in peace and security, those talents that hitherto they could exercise only in "countries which know not their language, and belong not to their race."[33]

Shortly before his death in 1930, Balfour told his niece, in his usual laconic manner, that "on the whole he felt that what he had been able to do for the Jews had been the thing he looked back upon as the most worth his doing." Weizmann was the last person, apart from the family, privileged enough to visit him at his deathbed. Balfour was too ill to speak, Weizmann too moved to do anything but weep.[34]

Balfour and Lloyd George—a very odd couple, who seemed to have little in common except their loyalty to the Zionist cause. Balfour may not have had warm personal relations with his colleagues—he was always described as reserved, aloof, detached—but no one questioned his utter rectitude and seriousness. That was not the case with Lloyd George. There may be no more scathing indictment of any English politician than John Maynard Keynes' portrait of Lloyd George. After paying tribute to his hard labor at the Versailles Conference, his hatred of war and "radical idealism," Keynes went on to describe the "Welsh Wizard," as he was known. "One catches in his company that flavor of final purposelessness, inner irresponsibility, existence outside or away from our Saxon good and evil, mixed with cunning, remorselessness, love of power."[35]

Yet this was the man who, with Balfour, shared a primary role in the passage of the Balfour Declaration. Some historians, like many of his contemporaries, regard Lloyd George's motives as entirely political and expediential. He himself gave that impression when he cynically said that "acetone converted me to Zionism," referring to the chemical process invented by Weizmann which was so useful in the war. (Weizmann himself disputed this, citing their warm relationship and many conversations about Zionism before that.)[36]* In his memoirs, Lloyd George also said that he intended the Declaration as a means of currying favor with Jewish financiers in the United States and Russian Jews who "wielded considerable influence in Bolshevik circles." But he wrote the memoirs, it has been pointed out, in the 1930s when the situation in Palestine was especially troublesome and he wanted to justify his support of Zionism without admitting to any sentimental or religious sentiments.[38]

Herbert Asquith, Prime Minister when the first draft of the Declaration was circulated (and who opposed it), said at the time that Lloyd George "does not care a damn for the Jews or their past or future but thinks it will be an outrage to let the Holy Places pass under the protectorate of 'agnostic, atheistic France'."[39]† But this says more about Asquith than about Lloyd George; even the reference to "agnostic, atheistic France" testifies to Lloyd George's religious disposition. Balfour, who knew him as well as anyone did, believed that the Old Testament was as much an abiding presence for Lloyd George as it was for him. Lloyd George himself said that when Weizmann talked to him about Palestine, "he kept bringing up place names which were more familiar to me than those of the Western front."[40] And not only place names, but the names of kings.

---

* This remark about acetone recalls Weizmann's first meeting with Churchill, then First Lord of the Admiralty, early in the war. Churchill's almost opening words were, "Well, Dr. Weizmann, we need thirty thousand tons of acetone. Can you make it?"[37]

† In 1915, Asquith had greeted with derision a proposal by Herbert Samuel (the first Jewish cabinet minister) for a Jewish Palestine: "It reads almost like a new edition of *Tancred* brought up to date. . . . It is a curious illustration of Dizzie's favorite dictum that 'race is everything' to find this almost lyrical outburst proceeding from the well-ordered and methodical brain of H.S."[39]

> I was brought up in a school where I was taught far more
> about the history of the Jews than about the history of
> my own land. I could tell you all the Kings of Israel. But I
> doubt whether I could have named half a dozen of the Kings
> of England and not more of the Kings of Wales. . . . On
> five days a week in the day school, and . . . in our Sunday
> schools, we were thoroughly versed in the history of the
> Hebrews.[41]

This education, the historian quoting this passage observes, left
Lloyd George with "an almost symbiotic sense of identity with
the People of the Book."[42]

Apart from the Biblical background that made those place
and kings so familiar to Lloyd George, there was another element that predisposed him to Zionism. This was the idea of
nationality—not English nationality but Welsh nationality, the
pride he had in his small nation, which for him had the fervor
of a religion. It was the threat to another small nation, Belgium,
that helped persuade him to abandon his anti-war position and
support Britain's entry into the war. And it was the appeal of yet
another small nation, Israel, that helped convert him to Zionism. Weizmann found, in conversations with him, that this was
their strong common ground. In the *Jewish Chronicle* in 1925,
Lloyd George told his Jewish audience:

> You belong to a very great race which has made the deepest
> impression upon the destinies of humanity. . . . We, the Welsh
> people, like you belong to a small race. . . . Your poets, kins
> and warriors are better known to the children and adults
> of Wales than are the names of our own heroes! . . . You
> call yourselves a small nation. I belong to a small nation,
> and I am proud of the fact. It is an ancient race, not as old
> as yours. . . . You may say you have been oppressed and

persecuted—that has been your power! You have been hammered into very fine steel, and that is why you can never be broken.[43]

In Jewish history, Lloyd George is remembered as the leader of the government that promulgated the Balfour Declaration which set Israel on the path to nationhood. In British history, he is remembered as the head of the government that saw Britain to victory in the First World War. One may also recall his speech, given early in the Second World War, that helped depose Chamberlain and bring in Churchill, the victor in yet another war, with momentous consequences for Israel as for the world.

Churchill: Philo-Zionist and Philosemite

It is interesting that the commanding figures in both world wars should have been philosemites of sorts, although of different backgrounds and political affiliations. Winston Churchill's father, Randolph, was, one might say, a "social" philosemite. He enjoyed the company and friendship of Jews (the Rothschilds, for example); he liked and admired Disraeli (as many in his party did not); and he respected the "race" that produced such admirable characters. His son Winston shared those traits. He came to know and respect not only the Jewish grandees but the less exalted Jews of Manchester, who made up almost a third of his constituency in 1906. Unlike Balfour, he opposed the Aliens Bill which would have restricted Jewish immigration; as one of his biographers wryly notes, his vote was surely "not unconnected with the fact that this was exactly when he alighted on Manchester North-West."[44] But it was more than political expediency that predisposed him to Zionism. Two years later, as Under-Secretary of State for the Colonies, he addressed the English Zionist Federation meeting in Manchester. "Jerusalem must be the ultimate goal," he told them. "*When* it will be achieved it is vain to prophesy; but that it will some day be achieved is one of the few certainties of the future."[45] Shortly afterwards, he lost his Manchester constituency and acquired a new one in Dundee, but he retained his pro-Jewish and pro-Zionist sentiments.

Churchill was not in the Cabinet that passed the Balfour Declaration, but he remained loyal to that Declaration after the war when Britain assumed the role of Mandate in Palestine. And he did so when he might easily have been provoked to turn against Zionism. Having the direst view of the Russian Revolution and of the Bolshevik-inspired movements throughout the world, he was distressed to find that Jews played a prominent part in both. His article in 1920, "Zionism versus Bolshevism: A Struggle for the Soul of the Jewish People," was a heartfelt attempt to come to terms with this dilemma. He opened with an encomium to the Jewish people, intended perhaps to mitigate the severe criticism that was to follow. "Some people like Jews and some do not; but no thoughtful man can doubt the fact that they are beyond all question the most formidable and the most remarkable race which has ever appeared in the world." He quoted Disraeli—"the Jew Prime Minister of England, . . . true to his race and proud of his origin"—as having said on a well-known occasion: "The Lord deals with the nations as the nations deal with the Jews." Churchill endorsed that sentiment. The Lord had inflicted on the Russian nation the evil of Bolshevism in return for the persecutions Russia had earlier inflicted on the Jews. Unfortunately, some Jews were now complicitous in that evil.

> We owe to the Jews in the Christian revelation a system
> of ethics which, even if it were entirely separated from the
> supernatural, would be incomparably the most precious

possession of mankind, worth in fact the fruits of all other wisdom and learning put together. On that system and by that faith there has been built out of the wreck of the Roman Empire the whole of our existing civilization. And it may well be that this same astounding race may at the present time be in the actual process of producing another system of morals and philosophy, as malevolent as Christianity was benevolent.

There were now three paths available to Jews: that of "national Jews" who are loyal citizens of the country in which they live (the English Jew, for example, who says, "I am an English man practising the Jewish faith"); that of "international Jews" (like many Russian Jews) who feel no loyalty either to their country or to their faith (they are atheists as well as revolutionaries); and that of Zionists who seek a national home for themselves and for other Jews in Palestine. The first and third paths are "helpful and hopeful," the second "absolutely destructive." National Jews could vindicate the honor of the Jewish name by combatting the Bolshevik conspiracy and being faithful to their adopted countries. And Zionists, with the help of the British government, could make that third alternative a reality by creating a Jewish national center in Palestine which would be not only a refuge for the oppressed but also "a symbol of Jewish unity and the temple of Jewish glory." If, as might well happen in his lifetime, Churchill predicted, a Jewish state under the protection of the British Crown were created, "an event would have occurred in the history of the world which would, from every point of view, be beneficial, and would be especially in harmony with the truest interests of the British Empire."[46]

Churchill's visit to Palestine the following year, during his brief tenure as Colonial Secretary, introduced him to the bitter reality of the situation—hostile Arabs confronting vigorous Jewish settlers. Before a crowd of ten thousand Jews at the site of the uncompleted Hebrew University on Mount Scopus, he delivered a speech declaring his "full sympathy for Zionism" and his belief that a Jewish national home in Palestine would be "a blessing to the whole world, a blessing to the Jewish race scattered all over the world, and a blessing to Great Britain." Britain's promise was two-fold: to help the Zionists and to assure the non-Jewish inhabitants that they would not suffer as a result. It was for the Zionists to see to it that everything they did was for the "moral and material benefit" of all Palestinians.[47] Responding to that plea, the Jews declared this was indeed their intention and expressed their gratitude to him for his support. They would have been pleased to know that when he met shortly afterwards with an Arab delegation, he rejected their principal demands: to deny the Jews a national home, to cease all immigration, and to establish a governing council elected only by those living in Palestine before the war. These proposals, he told them, would mean a repudiation of the Balfour Declaration, to which the British, and he himself, were unalterably committed.

Confronted with divided opinions within the government on the crucial subject of immigration, Churchill issued a White Paper in 1922 which did not set a quota for new Jewish immigrants to Palestine, as had been proposed, but did provide that their number be within the "economic absorptive capacity" of the country.[48] Zionists were displeased by this limitation but somewhat mollified by Churchill's reaffirmation of the Balfour Declaration and his assertion that Jews were in Palestine "as of right and not in sufferance."[49] After the fall of the government later that year and the end of his term as Colonial Secretary, his official involvement with Zionism came to an end for the rest of the decade.

In 1929, Churchill's period "in the wilderness" started (he was in Parliament but not in the Shadow Cabinet), as did his reengagement with Zionism. He made speech after speech defending the "national homeland," opposing proposals that would have given Arabs an absolute majority in a council and thus the ability to halt Jewish immigration, even anticipating an eventual "Jewish state." The Jews, he insisted, had brought to the Arabs "nothing but good gifts, more wealth, more trade, more civilisation, new sources of revenue, more employment, a higher rate of wages, larger cultivated areas and better water supply—in a word, the fruits of reason and modern science."[50] His Zionist zeal was reinforced by news about the persecution of Jews in Germany, which roused his fervor against Nazism and made a Jewish home in Palestine seem all the more imperative. Clement Attlee later recalled "the tears pouring down his cheeks one day before the war in the House of Commons, when he was telling me what was being done to the Jews in Germany—not to individual Jewish friends of his, but to the Jews as a group."[51]

A White Paper issued by Chamberlain in May 1939—dubbed by Zionists the "Black Paper"—set an absolute limit on Jewish immigration of 75,000 for five years, after which there would be no immigration unless the Arabs agreed to it. It also prohibited the sale of Arab land to Jews and envisioned an independent Arab state in ten years, without making mention of a Jewish state. In Parliament, Churchill vigorously attacked it as a violation of the Balfour Declaration, reminding Chamberlain that he himself had defended the Declaration in 1918, and that the British government was obliged to uphold it under the terms of the Mandate.

> This pledge of a home of refuge, of an asylum, was not made to the Jews in Palestine but to the Jews outside Palestine, to that vast, unhappy mass of scattered, persecuted, wandering Jews whose intense, unchanging, unconquerable desire has been for a National Home. . . . That is the pledge which was given, and that is the pledge which we are now asked to break, for how can this pledge be kept, I want to know, if in five years' time the National Home is to be barred and no more Jews are to be allowed in without the permission of the Arabs?

Repeating his by now familiar theme, he assured Parliament that the Arabs themselves benefited from the presence of the Jews. It was the Jews who "made the desert bloom, . . . started a score of of thriving industries, . . . founded a great city on the barren shore, . . . harnessed the Jordan and spread its electricity throughout the land." As a result, the Arab population in Palestine thrived and multiplied. All this would come to an end if the new White Paper were adopted, which was even more odious because the agitation for it was "fed with foreign money and ceaselessly inflamed by Nazi and by Fascist propaganda."

Those last words point to an issue that was never far from Churchill's consciousness in 1939. The pledge of a Jewish homeland in Palestine, he reminded Parliament, was a pledge made not only to Jews but to the world. And for the world, the new White Paper represented not only a repudiation of Britain's solemn obligation but also a confession of weakness. What would Britain's friends think of it? What the United States? And what, more fatally, its potential enemies?

Will they not be tempted to say: "They're on the run again. This is another Munich," and be the more stimulated in their aggression by these very unpleasant reflections which they may make?" May they be emboldened to take some irrevocable action and then find out, only after it is all too late, that it is not this Government, with their tired Ministers and flagging purpose, that they have to face, but the might of Britain and all that Britain means?[52]

"Your magnificent speech," Weizmann telegraphed him, "may yet destroy this policy."[53] That policy was not, however, destroyed. The White Paper remained in effect throughout the war, with the strong support of Parliament, the Cabinet, and, not least, the Colonial Office. Churchill's speech was delivered on May 23, 1939. A little more than four months later, Britain was at war, with Churchill in the Cabinet as First Lord of the Admiralty. The following May, he became Prime Minister. In 1943, when the issue arose again, he circulated that speech as a Cabinet paper, but the Cabinet was unmoved. Earlier, frustrated in his attempt to create a Jewish military force to fight with the Allied armies, he complained to Lord Cranborne, the Colonial Secretary, of the Colonial Office's "bias in favor of the Arabs and against the Jews." The Jews were in danger, he told him, and should be given the opportunity to defend themselves. "It may be necessary to make an example of these anti-Semitic officers, and others in high places. If three or four of them were recalled and dismissed, and the reasons given, it would have a salutary effect."[54] Cranborne, who shared that bias, was hardly disposed to act on that advice. In 1944, in a heated War Cabinet meeting about Hungarian Jews seeking refuge in Israel, Churchill declared that they had "as good a claim to Palestine" as Cranborne had to Hatfield (the long-time residence of the Cranbornes—that is, the Cecils.)[55]

With the establishment of the state of Israel in 1948, Churchill, no longer in office, started another campaign, this time to recognize the state. On January 26, 1949, in a debate on foreign policy in the House, he pointed out that it was nine months since the establishment of the state, which had been recognized, on that very day, by both the United States and the Soviet Union, and since then by a dozen or more nations. The delay on the part of Britain, he suspected, was due to "the very strong and direct streak of bias and prejudice on the part of the Foreign Secretary" (Ernest Bevin). In defense of the new state, he invoked his usual argument about the Jews "making the desert bloom," which already had the effect of doubling the population of both Jews and Arabs and which had a limitless potentiality for growth. The heart of the speech, however, was the appeal to the verdict of history.

> The coming into being of a Jewish state in Palestine is an
> event in world history to be viewed in the persepective,
> not of a generation or a century, but in the perspective of a
> thousand, two thousand or even three thousand years. That
> is a standard of temporal values or time-values which seems
> very much out of accord with the perpetual click-clack of
> our rapidly changing moods and of the age in which we live.
> This is an event in world history.[56]

Nine days after this debate in Parliament, Britain formally recognized the state of Israel—not, probably, as a result of Churchill's intervention, although Israel was grateful to him. To the letter of thanks by Weizmann, Israel's first president, Churchill replied that he looked back with pleasure to their long association, adding, somewhat elliptically, "The light grows."[57]

After yet another term as Prime Minister in 1951, Churchill retired in 1955. The following year, on the eve of the Suez crisis, he urged President Eisenhower not to stand by while Israel was defeated by Russian arms. He himself had no doubt about the merits of the case: "I am, of course, a Zionist, and have been ever since the Balfour Declaration. I think it is a wonderful thing that this tiny colony of Jews should have become a refuge to their compatriots in all the lands where they were persecuted so cruelly, and at the same time established themselves as the most effective fighting force in the area."[58]

Churchill's philo-Zionism—and philosemitism—had everything to do with that "event in world history" and very little with religion, except in so far as he recognized Judaism as a moral and civilizing force in history. In 1953, in the unlikely context of his book on the Second World War, he reflected upon the two "races," the Jews and the Greeks, who, above all others, had set their mark upon the world. "No two cities have counted more with mankind than Athens and Jerusalem. Their messages in religion, philosophy, and art have been the main guiding lights of modern faith and culture." He himself was "on the side of both, and believed in their invincible power to survive internal strife and the world tides threatening their extinction."[59]*

These passing references to "religion" and "faith" have none of the passion other philosemites brought to those terms. Shaftesbury would have been appalled, and Balfour and Lloyd George perhaps amused but also discomfited, by the irreverence of Churchill's famous quip, toward the end of his life: "I am ready to meet my Maker. Whether my Maker is ready to meet me is another question." Asked to elaborate on his religious belief, he quoted a character in one of Disraeli's novels, "Sen-

---

* In the same passage, praising the Greeks and Jews for the vigor of their political life and strife, Churchill tossed off another of his quips: "It has been well said that wherever there are three Jews it will be found that there are two Prime Ministers and one leader of the Opposition."

sible men are all of the same religion." Pressed further, he cited Disraeli again, "Sensible men never tell."[60]*

One of the rare occasions when Churchill dwelt at any length on a religious theme was in 1931 in an article in a Sunday newspaper. "Moses: The Leader of a People" opens with an epigraph from Deuteronomy:

> And there arose not a prophet since in Israel like unto
> Moses, whom the Lord knew face to face, in all the signs
> and the wonders, which the Lord sent him to do in the land
> of Egypt to Pharaoh, and to all his servants, and to all his
> land, and in all that mighty hand, and in all the great terror
> which Moses showed in the sight of all Israel.

The epigraph, Churchill explained, was "an apt expression of the esteem in which the great leader and liberator of the Hebrew people was held by the generations that succeeded him." "Esteem," not "veneration." In that prosaic style, Churchill went on to relate the story of Moses, with only a very occasional hint of his usual wit or irony.†

> He [Moses] was the greatest of the prophets, who spoke in
> person to the God of Israel; he was the national hero who led
> the Chosen People out of the land of bondage, through the
> perils of the wilderness, and brought them to the very thresh-
> hold of the Promised Land; he was the supreme law-giver,

---

* The "sensible men" quip comes from Disraeli's novel *Endymion*, but it did not originate with him. It was used almost a century earlier by the First Earl of Shaftesbury, who called for a "good humored religion" that would depend not on the "higher regions of divinity" but on "plain honest morals."[61]

† One display of irreverence was prompted by the Biblical account of the crossing of the Red Sea—600,000, plus women and children. "We may," Churchill commented, "without impiety doubt the statistics. A clerical error may so easily have arisen. Even today a nought or two is sometimes misplaced."

who received from God that remarkable code upon which the
religious, moral, and social life of the nation was so securely
fashioned. Tradition lastly ascribed to him the authorship of
the whole Pentateuch, and the mystery that surrounded his
death added to his prestige.

Again, "prestige," like "esteem"—terms more suitable to a
politician than to "the greatest of prophets." Only toward the
end of the article did religion make a more serious appearance
when Churchill took issue with the scientists and rationalists
who denied the Biblical miracles and made of Moses a legend-
ary figure embodying the moral and religious precepts of the
people. In fact, he insisted, the essential truths of the Biblical
story had been affirmed: "This wandering tribe . . . grasped and
proclaimed an idea of which all the genius of Greece and all
the power of Rome were incapable. There was to be only one
God, a universal God, a God of nations, a just God, a God who
would punish in another world a wicked man." Almost as an
afterthought, he invoked the Christian God who brought "a
new revelation" inspired by the "Hebrew people"—"a God not
only of justice, but of mercy; a God not only of self-preservation
and survival, but of pity, self-sacrifice, and ineffable love."[62]
It was in November 1931 that Churchill wrote this curious bit of Biblical exegesis. His party was out of power and
he himself, disagreeing with Baldwin on the subject of India,
had resigned from the Shadow Cabinet a few months earlier.
He was now truly "in the wilderness," out of favor even in his
own party. It is hard to resist the thought that he saw the Moses
parable as specially relevant to him. "Every prophet," he wrote
midway in the essay, "has to come from civilization, but every
prophet has to go into the wilderness. He must have a strong
impression of a complex society and all that it has to give, and
then he must serve periods of isolation and meditation. This

is the process by which psychic dynamite is made."[63] Even Churchill was not vainglorious enough to suppose that he was the prophet chosen to lead the English people out of the wilderness. But he might well have thought that, by that process of "psychic dynamite," he himself might be led out of the wilderness, bringing his people with him.

And so it was. A decade later, as Prime Minister, he was leading his country through the perils of another wilderness. Two-thirds of a century later, a review of Martin Gilbert's *Churchill and the Jews* bore the headline, "Winston Churchill: A Latter-Day Moses?" The question mark suggests the reviewer's doubts not only about Churchill's right to claim that legacy, but also the degree of his devotion to Jews. Yet the review opens by recalling the remark of one of Churchill's friends: "Even Winston had a fault. He was too fond of Jews."[64]

"Too fond of Jews," that is one way to characterize Churchill's philosemitism—a love, not uncritical on occasion and sometimes distracted or compromised by political pressures, but deeply held and memorably expressed. Churchill was surely no Moses, no savior of the Jews (although some acclaim him a savior of Western civilization). But in that "event in world history" which he so often spoke of, the establishment of the state of Israel, he has an honorable place. And in the civilization that he so prized, it was no small tribute to Jerusalem to be put on a par with Athens as the guiding lights of mankind.

Epilogue

If the history of philosemitism may recall England to its "past glory," it may also recall Jews to a glory they themselves tend to forget. In this sense, it is more than a counter-history to anti-semitism. It is a history in its own right. While many English philosemites felt obliged to confront and refute the familiar antisemitic gibes, they did so almost as an afterthought, as the protagonists in a debate. But many did not feel the need to do even that. They were not simply reacting to others; they were speaking in their own voice and for their own purpose—which may inspire Jews to speak for themselves, not defensively but proudly. If Lionel Trilling found even in the "counter-myths" of fiction some reality, "a little of what is true," so Jews may find, even in the extravagant tributes of philosemites, something true.[1]

Jews may be reminded of what it is that many philosem-ites found so commendable in the Jewish "race." That word is anathema today. Yet in that time and context, it was meant as a tribute, denoting a people with an ancient lineage, a spiritual blood-line, as it were. When Lloyd George spoke of the Jewish race, it was in the same spirit that he praised the Welsh as an "ancient race"; and so with Churchill, who as late as 1954, was proud of the English, as a "race dwelling all around the globe."[2] The Jewish race, as both recognized, was different from the others—more ancient than the Welsh, and more dispersed than the English. Today we would translate "Jewish race" as "Jewish people"—again, with the proviso that they are a people unlike others, not only more ancient and more dispersed but also heirs to the most venerable of religions.

This is one of the many ironies of modern Jewish history. The Enlightenment has been, in important ways, a boon to Jewry, relieving them of the persecution and discrimination that have blighted so much of their history. Yet some of the most estimable figures of the Enlightenment, the *philosophes*, in their zeal for reason, were hostile not only to Judaism as a religion, the *fons et origo* of Christianity, but also to Jews as individuals who were so benighted as to adhere to that outmoded and regressive faith, and, worse, to the Jewish people as a "nation within a nation," a discordant element in an otherwise united and enlightened society. Philosemites, on the other hand, not always "enlightened" by conventional standards, have respected, even revered, the Jewish religion as the unique and essential nature of the Jewish people, the cause of their survival, and ultimately the reason for their restoration to their ancient land. The Jews as "the people of the Book," "God's ancient people," "the chosen people," "the apple of God's eye"—these are the recurrent motifs in the rhetoric of Christian philosemites, who esteemed Judaism precisely because they esteemed Christianity.

From millenarianism to Evangelicalism, from philosemitism to philo-Zionism—this too reminds us of a history we tend to forget. The horrendous facts of the Holocaust induce a foreshortening of memory, suggesting that Zionism was a response to the Holocaust and Israel a haven for refugees and potential refugees. But long before the Holocaust, Zionism (although not under that label) and Israel (otherwise known as Palestine) inspired Christians as well as Jews, and for different reasons. Millenarians and Evangelicals favored the "restoration" of the Jews to the "holy land" as the precondition of their own redemption, while others sought the establishment of a Jewish state as the fulfillment of a Biblical prophecy and command. Mordecai's fantasy, expressed so graphically by George Eliot, was of a wandering "soul" of medieval sages and poets which could find a resting place only in Palestine. Balfour made the point less dramatically when he said that Palestine, rather than Uganda, was the only home for Jews because it was there that "that race was nurtured and that religion came into being." So, too, Churchill insisted that Jews were in Palestine "as of right and not in sufferance"—not merely by the legal right of the Mandate, but by the historic right of that ancient people.[3]

Some of the tributes of the English philosemites are too heady for modern Jews: Ashley's praise of the Jews as "the most remarkable nation that had ever yet appeared on the face of earth," or Churchill, unwittingly echoing him, who said that whether one liked Jews or not, no one could doubt that they were "the most formidable and the most remarkable race which has ever appeared in the world."[4] Philosemitism may seem too exuberant—irrationally exuberant, in the case of Ashley, who extolled the Jews even while opposing their admission to Parliament. If many American Jews, including Zionists, are wary of Evangelicals, who are among their most faithful allies, it is not only, as is often said, because Jews remember all too well the saga of persecution at the hands of Christians, but also because they are distrustful of any religious zealotry, on the part of Christians or, more ominously today, of Muslims.

Jews may be flattered by the philosemitic enthusiasm of Eliot or Churchill. But they are more comfortable with the restrained, prosaic, matter-of-fact toleration accorded them by Locke or Macaulay. One might say of the idea of toleration what Tocqueville said of self-interest: "The principle of toleration rightly understood is not a lofty one, but it is clear and sure. It does not aim at mighty objects, but it attains without excessive exertion all those at which it aims." Toleration is surely less lofty than philosemitism, but it is more "clear and sure"—witness Macaulay's arguments in favor of, and Ashley's opposed to, the admission of Jews in Parliament.

In the course of the history of Anglo-Jewry—from the readmission of the Jews in England, to their admission in Parliament, and beyond that to the founding of the state of Israel—the principles of philosemitism and toleration played different roles at different times, but always in a common cause. In fiction it was philosemitism that prevailed, presenting images of Jews and ideas of Judaism that counteracted the familiar stereotypes and created more favorable, even exalted ones. In politics, it was the principle of toleration that finally bestowed upon Jews the "rights and privileges" of citizenship, not because they were superior beings (the "chosen people"), but because they were human beings, like all Englishmen. And it was the combination of these principles that inspired the idea of a Jewish state—for some a "holy land" for a "holy people," for others a nation like unto all nations.

If the history of antisemitism is too "lachrymose," the history of philosemitism may seem too Pollyannaish. And so perhaps it is, on its own. But it is not on its own. There is that other counter-history it is always contending with, the all-too-persistent antisemitism resurgent today. It may be appropriate that the present study of philosemitism has taken the modest form of an essay rather than a history proper, whereas antisemitism, now more than ever, warrants nothing less than a massive tome. Yet even an essay may provide a respite from the dismal reality, a reminder of a "past glory" that is still resonant in the present and gives us hope for the future.

My brother Milton Himmelfarb, in one of his last essays, reflected on the question, "What do I believe?" He concluded by quoting the Israeli anthem *Hatikvah*, "Our hope is not lost." Those words, he reminds us, were an answer to the contemporaries of Ezekiel, who, more than two and a half millennia ago, had despaired, "Our hope is lost." "Hope," Himmelfarb observes, "is a Jewish virtue."[5]

Notes

Prologue

1. Jean-Paul Sartre, *Anti-Semite and Jew*, trans. George J. Becker (New York, 1948), pp. 143, 150.

2. Salo Baron, "Ghetto and Emancipation: Shall We Revise the Traditional View," *Menorah Journal*, June 1928. This "lachrymose view" has also been disputed by Jonathan Sacks, the Chief Rabbi of Great Britain. See the prologue to *Future Tense: Jews, Judaism, and Israel in the Twenty-First Century* (New York, 2009).

3. Emil L. Fackenheim, *To Mend the World: Foundations of Future Jewish Thought* (New York, 1982), p. 299. See also *The Jewish Return into History* (New York, 1978).

4. Robert S. Wistrich, *A Lethal Obsession: Anti-Semitism from Antiquity to the Global Jihad* (New York, 2010); Anthony Julius, *Trials of the Diaspora: A History of Anti-Semitism in England* (Oxford, 2010); and Melanie Phillips, *The World Turned Upside Down: The Global Battle over God, Truth, and Power* (New York, 2010).

5. William D. Rubinstein and Hilary L. Rubinstein, *Philosemitism: Admiration and Support in the English-Speaking World for Jews, 1840–1939* (London, 1999), p. 189.

6. William D. Rubinstein, *Israel, the Jews and the West: The Fall and Rise of Antisemitism* (London, 2008).

7. Julius, p. xxxvii.

8. Heinrich von Treitschke, "A Word About Our Jewry" (1880) (reproduced on the Internet); "Philosemitism" in *Encyclopedia of Christianity*, ed. Erwin Fahlbusch and G. W. Bromley.

9. The 1888 volume of the *Oxford English Dictionary* cites examples of "antisemitism" in 1881 and 1882 (not as a separate entry but under the prefix "anti-"). But "philosemitism" does not appear, even as a prefix, in the 1909 volume. In the 1989 edition, "philo-Semitism" appears as a prefix, the first example dating from 1946. In the 2008 edition, both "antisemitism" and "philosemitism" are elevated to the status of entries, citing earlier examples of "philo-semitic" in 1881 and 1891.

10. The word "philosemitic" appears in 1934 in one of Cecil Roth's earliest books, *The Life of Menasseh ben Israel*. One chapter of his seminal work, *A History of the Jews in England*, in 1941, opens by referring to the "unmistakable philosemitic tendency in certain English circles." In his essay, "England in Jewish History" (1949), he speaks of the "strong philosemitic movement in the country" even before the readmission of the Jews. (He also cites an essay by a German historian the preceding year, "*Der Philosemitismus des 17' Jahrhunderts.*") His 1949 essay was reprinted in 1962, under the title "Philo-Semitism in England," in his volume, *Essays and Portraits in Anglo-Jewish History.* Oddly still, Roth is not among those cited in the three references to the word in the index of the latest edition of the *Encyclopaedia Judaica*.

11. Quoted by Adam Sutcliffe, "Enlightenment and Exclusion: Judaism and Toleration in Spinoza, Locke and Bayle," in *Philosemitism, Antisemitism and 'the Jews'*," ed. Tony Kushner and Nadia Val-

man (Hampshire, Eng., 2004) p. 193. The comment on toleration appears in Goethe's *Nachlass*. For Hegel's admiration for Goethe, see Walter Kaufman, *Hegel: Reinterpretation, Texts, and Commentary* (New York, 1965), pp. 45–6.

12. Koran, 3:199.

13. Koran, 3:70–71.

14. Quoted by Douglas J. Culver, *Albion and Ariel: British Puritanism and the Birth of Zionism* (New York, 1995), p. 54. Timothy Larsen's *A People of One Book: The Bible and the Victorians*, has a more limited scope. For most of the Victorians he discusses—Anglo-Catholics, Roman Catholics, Unitarians—the "book" was largely the New Testament.

15. See below, p. 81.

16. See below, p. 122.

17. Todd Endelman, *Jews of Georgian England, 1714–1830: Tradition and Change in a Liberal Society* (Phila., 1979), p. 17.

18. Julius, pp. 38–41.

19. Benjamin Disraeli, *Coningsby, or the New Generation* (*Works*, London, n.d.), pp. 249–52.

20. Winston Churchill, "Zionism versus Bolshevism: A Struggle for the Soul of the Jewish People," *Illustrated Sunday Herald*, Feb. 8, 1920. See below, p. 139.

21. William and Hilary Rubinstein, *Philosemitism*, p. 168. See below, p. 152.

22. Martin Gilbert, "The Origins of the 'Iron Curtain' Speech," in *Winston Churchill: Resolution, Defiance, Magnanimity, Good Will*, ed. R. Crosby Kemper III (Columbia, Mo., 1996), p. 49.

I. In the Beginning

1. Winston Churchill, *A History of the English-Speaking Peoples* (New York, 1956), I, 290.

2.   Douglas J. Culver, *Albion and Ariel: British Puritanism and the Birth of Political Zionism* (New York, 1995), p. 54 (quoting John Richard Green, *Short History of the English People*).

3.   Adam Sutcliffe, *Judaism and Enlightenment* (Camb., Eng., 2003), p. 46. Sutcliffe makes a large point of the decline of the importance of Hebraism by the early eighteenth century, although the echoes of it can be heard well into the nineteenth. On the scholarly controversy about Hebraism, see Eric Nelson, *The Hebrew Republic: Jewish Sources and the Transformation of European Political Thought* (Cambridge, Mass., 2010, and the review essay by Yoram Hazony, "The Biblical Century," *Azure*, Summer 2010, pp. 118–28.

4.   Thomas Hobbes, *Leviathan* (London, 1914), p. 222 (part 3, chap. 35), and p. 234 (chap. 36).

5.   Culver, pp. 108–9. (I have modernized the spelling of the title as well as of the quotations.)

6.   Adam Sutcliffe, "Enlightenment and Exclusion: Judaism and Toleration in Spinoza, Locke, and Bayle," in Tony Kushner and Nadia Valman, eds., *Philosemitism, Antisemitism and 'the Jews'* (Hampshire, Eng., 2004), p. 179. "The apple of God's eye" was a familiar quotation from the Bible (*Deuteronomy*, 32:10).

7.   Roger Williams, *The Bloudy Tenent of Persecution* (reproduced on the Internet), p. 1.

8.   Williams, chap. LXX.

9.   Eliane Glaser, *Judaism Without Jews: Philosemitism and Christian Polemic in Early Modern England* (London, 2007), p. 95.

10. David S. Katz, *Philo-Semitism and the Readmission of the Jews to England, 1603–1655* (Oxford, 1982), pp. 181–2. This was not the Sir Edward Nicholas who was Secretary of State under Charles II. Cecil Roth suggests that the tract was perhaps written by a Jew or translated by Menasseh ben Israel. Roth, *A History of the Jews in England* (3d ed., London, 1964 [1st ed., 1941]), p. 286, note d; Roth, *Essays and Portraits in Anglo-Jewish History* (Phila., 1962), p. 88.

11. Cecil Roth, *History*, pp. 149–50; David S. Katz, *The Jews in the History of England, 1485–1850* (Oxford, 1994), p. 114. Both apply the term "philosemitic" to the Hebraic and millenarian movements, but they disagree on the other motives attributed to Cromwell. Katz minimizes the importance of both the economic factor and the idea of toleration. (Unless otherwise specified, other references to Katz are to *The Jews in the History of England*.)

12. Churchill, II, pp. 303, 315.

13. Roth, *History*, pp. 153–4; Barbara W. Tuchman, *Bible and Sword: England and Palestine from the Bronze Age to Balfour* (New York, 1956), p. 121. See also Roth, "Philosemitism in England" (1949) and "The Mystery of the Resettlement" (1956), in *Essays*.

14. Roth, *Essays*, p. 91.

15. Thomas Carlyle, *Oliver Cromwell's Letters and Speeches* (New York, 1845), II, pp. 51–2.

16. Roth, *History*, p. 161; Katz, p. 117.

17. Katz, p. 127.

18. Roth, *Essays*, p. 96; Katz, p. 126.

19. Avrom Saltman, *The Jewish Question in 1655: Studies in Prynne's Demurrer* (Jerusalem, 1995), p. 19; Roth, *History*, p. 162. In spite of Prynne's "declared hostility to the Jews," Katz says, his book was not at all the "hysterical denunciation of the Jews" it is sometimes made out to be, and remains "a faithful compilation of the materials available in his day for a history of the Jews in England" (Katz, pp. 129–30).

20. Saltman, pp. 19–20, 43.

21. Carlyle, II, 201; Katz, pp. 130–1. Carlyle dates that closing event as December 12, but other sources give it as the 18th.

22. Roth, *History*, p. 166.

23. Katz, p. 132.

24. On the fallacy of "Whig history," see Katz, pp. vii, 383. Eliane Glaser refers to it as "teleological history" (*Judaism Without Jews*, pp. 3, 27, 132).

25. Peter H. Marshall, *William Godwin* (New Haven, Conn., 1984), p. 359; Glaser, p. 21. The biography of Cromwell by John Morley (himself a good liberal) presents much the same view of Cromwell, commending him for adhering to the principle of toleration, "with the two stereotyped exclusions of popery and prelacy." (Morley, *Oliver Cromwell* [New York, 1901], p. 367.)

26. Clay Javier Boggs, "'The Jews' and 'the Pharisees' in Early Quaker Polemic," April 6, 2007 (reproduced on the Internet). Boggs (a Quaker and a professor of history at Temple University) quotes at length from Fox's tract "Saul's Errand to Damascus." On Margaret Fell, Fox's wife, see Claire Jowett, "'Inward' and 'Outward' Jews: Margaret Fell, Circumcision nd Women's Preaching," in Kushner and Valman, eds., pp. 155–76.

27. Jason P. Rosenblatt, *Renaissance England's Chief Rabbi: John Selden* (Oxford, 2006).

28. *New Atlantis*, reproduced on the Internet.

29. Lewis Feuer, "Francis Bacon and the Jews: Who Was the Jew in the *New Atlantis?*," *Jewish Historical Studies of England*, XXIX (1982–86), 1–25.

30. James Harrington, *Commonwealth of Oceana* (reproduced on the Internet), pp. 49 and ff. See also the account of Harrington in Jonathan Karp, "The Mosaic Republic in Augustan Politics: John Toland's 'Reasons for Naturalizing the Jews'," *Hebraic Political Studies*, Summer 2006.

31. Harrington, *Oceana*, p. 184. In an otherwise fine biography of Harrington by Charles Blitzer, *An Immortal Commonwealth: The Political Thought of James Harrington* (New Haven, 1960), in the almost seventy-page chapter on *Oceana*, Panopea and the Jews are mentioned only in a single long footnote (p. 215), and without the concluding sentence. Karp's essay on Toland is one of the few to do justice to this subject.

32. Harrington, p. 49.

33. John Milton, "Areopagitica" (1644), in *Milton's Prose Writings*, ed. K. M. Burton (London, 1958), p. 182.

34. Samuel S. Stollman, "Milton's Dichotomy of 'Judaism' and 'Hebraism'," *PMLA*, Jan. 1974, pp. 105–12.

35. Stollman, passim; and Achsah Guibbory, "England, Israel, and the Jews in Milton's Prose, 1649–1660," in *Milton and the Jews*, ed. Douglas A. Brooks (Camb., Eng., 2008), pp. 13–34.

36. John Milton, "The Ready and Easy Way to Establish a Free Commonwealth" (April 1660), in *Milton's Prose Writings*, p. 243.

37. Stollman, p. 106 (quoting Milton, *The Christian Doctrine*, XIV, 29).

38. Milton, "The Doctrine and Discipline of Divorce" (1643), in *Milton's Prose Writings*, p. 289; Nicholas von Maltzahn, "Making Use of the Jews: Milton and Philo-Semitism," in *Milton and the Jews*, p. 72.

39. Guibbory, pp. 18, 34. (Italics in the original.)

40. Basil Willey, *The Seventeenth Century Background: Studies in the Thought of the Age in Relation to Poetry and Religion* (New York, 1953), p. 219.

II. The Case for Toleration

1. Cecil Roth, *A History of the Jews in England* (3d ed., Oxf., 1964), p. 171.

2. Roth, p. 183.

3. *Diary of Samuel Pepys* (London, 1906), I, 414 (Oct. 14, 1663).

4. John Locke, *Two Treatises of Government* and *A Letter Concerning Toleration*, ed. Ian Shapiro (New Haven, Conn., 2003), pp. 245–6. Among those who interpret Locke as denying toleration to Catholics and atheists are two of the commentators in this edition, Ian Shapiro and John Dunn (pp. , xiii, 276, 319). See also Perez Zagorin,

How the Idea of Toleration Came to the West (Princeton, 2003), p. 264; and Adam Sutcliffe, "Enlightenment and Exclusion: Judaism and Toleration in Spinoza, Locke and Bayle," in Tony Kushner and Nadia Valman, eds., *Philosemitism, Antisemitism and 'the Jews'* (Hampshire, Eng., 2004). For the argument against this limited view of toleration, see Adam Wolfson, *Persecution and Toleration: An Explication of the Locke-Proast Quarrel, 1689–1704* (Lanham, Md., 2010).

5.   Locke, *Letter Concerning Toleration*, p. 246.

6.   Locke, p. 220.

7.   Locke, pp. 240–1.

8.   Locke, pp. 249–50.

9.   The publication date of *Two Treaties* is generally given as 1690, which was the date that appeared in the book itself. In fact, it was on sale as early as October 1689 and was deliberately post-dated by the publisher. (Maurice Cranston, *John Locke: A Biography* [London, 1957], p. 327.)

10.   The strongest case for the secularist interpretation of the *Treatises* and of Locke in general is Leo Strauss's *Natural Right and History* (Chicago, 1953), pp. 202–51. For recent discussion of this issue, see Fania Oz-Salzberger, "The Political Thought of John Locke and the Significance of Political Hebraism," *Hebraic Political Studies*, Fall 2006, pp. 568–92; and Andrew Rehfeld, "Jephthah, the Hebrew Bible, and John Locke's 'Second Treatise of Government'," *Hebraic Political Studies*, Winter 2008, pp. 60–93.

11.   David S. Katz, *The Jews in the History of England, 1485–1850* (Oxford, 1994), p. 236.

12.   Frank E. Manuel, *The Religion of Isaac Newton: The Fremantle Lectures* (Oxford, 1974); and Manuel, *The Broken Staff: Judaism Through Christian Eyes* (Cambridge, Mass., 1992), pp. 147–48.

13.   Winston S. Churchill, *A History of the English-Speaking Peoples* (New York, 1957), III, 105.

14.   Roth, pp. 203–4.

15. Linda Colley, *Britons: Forging the Nation, 1707–1837* (New Haven, Conn., 1992), pp. 30–31.

16. On the word "race," see Prologue above, p. 8.

17. Joseph Addison, "The Race of People called Jews," in *The Spectator*, Sept. 27, 1712.

18. *Spectator*, March 12, 1711.

19. Jonathan Karp, "The Mosaic Republic in Augustan Politics: John Toland's 'Reasons for Naturalizing the Jews'," *Hebraic Political Studies*, Summer 2006, p. 470.

20. Karp, p. 490.

21. Karp, p. 485.

22. Manuel, *Broken Staff*, p. 125.

23. Diego Lucci, "Judaism and the Jews in the British Deists' Attacks on Revealed Religion," *Hebraic Political Studies*, Spring 2008, pp. 206–7.

24. Thomas W. Perry, *Public Opinion, Propaganda, and Politics in Eighteenth-Century England: A Study of the Jew Bill of 1753* (Cambridge, Mass., 1962), p. 55.

25. On the "Jewish Question" in Germany in the nineteenth century, see Gertrude Himmelfarb, *The Jewish Odyssey of George Eliot* (New York, 2009), pp. 18–26.

26. Perry, p. 74.

27. Perry, pp. 74–5. For Perry the party struggle was the main factor in this event, as in English history in general at this time. One of the purposes of his book on the Jew Bill is to dispute Sir Lewis Namier, who made light of the importance of parties in this period.

28. Perry, p. 135; Roth, p. 221.

29. Perry, p. 145.

30. Élie Halévy, *England in 1815*, tr. E. I. Watkin and D. A. Barker (London, 1960 [1st ed. in French, 1913]), p. 148.

31. Horace Walpole, *Memoirs of the Reign of King George the Second* (2d ed., London, 1846), I, 357–8. (I am indebted to Katz, p. 240, for alerting me to this source.)

32. For these figures, see Perry, p. 5; Katz, pp. 250, 292, 317.

33. Adam Smith, *Lectures on Jurisprudence*, ed. R. L. Meek, D. D. Raphael, and P. G. Stein (Oxford, 1978), pp. 527–8 (Report of 1766).

34. Smith, p. 527.

35. Burke, *Reflections on the Revolution in France* (New York, Dolphin ed., 1961), pp. 60–1, 67, 97–8.

36. Burke, p. 97.

37. *The Speeches of the Right Honourable Edmund Burke in the House of Commons and in Westminster Hall* (London, 1816), II, 250–51. (William D. Rubinstein and Hilary L. Rubinstein, *Philosemitism: Admiration and Support in the English-Speaking World for Jews, 1840–1939* [London, 1999], pp. 173–4, called my attention to this speech.) I have found no evidence of how the motion was received or resolved in Parliament.

38. Burke, *Reflections*, p. 165. The *Reflections*, I have elsewhere argued, may be taken not as a vindication of Jews as such but rather of Judaism as a religion. (Gertrude Himmelfarb, "Edmund Burke: Apologist for Judaism?" in *The Moral Imagination: From Edmund Burke to Lionel Trilling* [Chicago, 2006], pp. 3–11.)

39. Todd M. Endelman, *The Jews of Georgian England, 1714–1830: Tradition and Change in a Liberal Society* (Philadelphia, 1979), p. 48.

40. Roth, pp. 234–38.

III. The Case for Political Equality

1. C. C. N. Salbstein, *The Emancipation of the Jews in Britain: The Question of the Admission of the Jews to Parliament, 1828–1860* (East Brunswick, N.J., 1982), p. 44.

2. On the technicalities of the electoral laws, see H. S. Q. Henriques, *The Jews and the English Law* (1908).

3.   Robert Grant, speech in the House of Commons, April 5, 1830 (All the speeches cited in this chapter are from Hansard's Parliamentary Debates, reproduced on the Internet).

4.   Robert Inglis, speech in the House of Common, April 5, 1830.

5.   *The Life and Letters of Lord Macaulay*, ed. G. Otto Trevelyan (New York, 1875), I, 146 (to Macvey Napier, Jan. 25, 1830)

6.   Macaulay, speech in the House of Commons, April 5, 1830.

7.   Macaulay, speech in the House of Commons, April 5, 1830.

8.   Macaulay, *Life and Letters*, I, 152.

9.   John Clive, *Macaulay: The Shaping of the Historian* (New York, 1973), p. 158.

10.   Macaulay, "Civil Disabilities of the Jews," *Edinburgh Review*, January 1831.

11.   Macaulay, speech in the House of Commons, April 17, 1833, in *The Works of Lord Macaulay*, ed. by his sister, Lady Trevelyan (8 vol. ed., London, 1875), VIII, 110.

12.   William Hazlitt, "Emancipation of the Jews" (1831), in *Collected Works*, ed. A. R. Waller and Arnold Glover (London, 1904), XII, 461–2, 466. The phrase, "vulgar prejudices," was used repeatedly in the eighteenth as well as nineteenth century to refer to antisemites. See, for example, John Toland (pp. 43–45) and Horace Walpole (p. 50).

13.   John O. Osborne, *William Cobbett: His Thought and his Times* (New Brunswick, N. J., 1966), pp. 222–23; George Spater, *William Cobbett: The Poor Man's Friend* (Camb., Eng., 1982), II, 441, 591, n. 79. Osborne is candid about Cobbett's antisemitism, describing it as "so extreme, it resembled a parody. It was never qualified and was expressed in the grossest terms," such as admiring the persecution of the Jews in the Middle Ages (p. 222). Spater refers to his antisemitism only in passing twice in the text, with a few other examples in endnotes. He says that Cobbett disclaimed any intention to

persecute the Jews, only not to encourage them, as that would be a "blasphemy" (II, 41). The suggestion that the Jews be banished from England appears in an endnote. That note concludes, without further elaboration: "After C's breakdown in 1833, he became increasingly antisemitic" (II, 591, n. 79). Anthony Julius, in *Trials of the Diaspora: A History of Anti-Semitism in England* (Oxford, 2010), cites other biographers who have neglected or trivialized Cobbett's antisemitism (p. 402, and notes 339–41, p. 717).

14. James Anthony Froude, *Thomas Carlyle: A History of His Life in London, 1834–1881* (London, 1884), II, 448–9.

15. Abigail Green, *Moses Montefiore: Jewish Liberator, Imperial Hero* (Camb., Mass., 2010), pp. 110–11.

16. Russell, speech in the House of Commons, Dec. 16, 1847.

17. John Morley, *The Life of William Ewart Gladstone* (3 vols., New York, 1903), I, 376.

18. Gladstone, speech in the House of Commons, Dec. 16, 1847.

19. Benjamin Disraeli, *Tancred, or the New Crusade* (*Collected Works*, London, n.d. [1st ed., 1847]), p. 196. See below, p. 96.

20. Disraeli, speech in the House of Commons, Dec. 16, 1847.

21. On Disraeli's situation at the time, see William Flavelle Monypenny and George Earle Buckle, *The Life of Benjamin Disraeli* (2 vol. ed., London, 1929), I, 894; Robert Blake, *Disraeli* (London, 1966), p. 260.

22. See below, chapter V.

23. Lord Ashley, speech in the House of Commons, Dec. 16, 1847.

24. John Stuart Mill, "The Attempt to Exclude Unbelievers from Parliament," *Daily News*, March 26, 1849, in Mill, *Newspaper Writings*, ed. Ann P. Robson and John M. Robson (Toronto, 1986), IV, 1136–37 (in *Collected Works*, XXV).

25. John Stuart Mill, *Considerations on Representative Government* (in *Utilitarianism, Liberty, and Representative Government*, London 1910), p. 201.

26. Edwin Hodder, *The Life and Work of the Seventh Earl of Shaftesbury* (London, 1888), p. 553 (diary, July 1, 1858).

27. Hodder, p. 632 (letter to Gladstone, Dec. 22, 1868).

28. Gertrude Himmelfarb, *The Jewish Odyssey of George Eliot* (New York, 2009), pp. 15–16.

29. Arthur P. Stanley, *Life and Correspondence of Thomas Arnold* (New York, 1910), I, 333 (letter to Rev. Julius Hare, May 12, 1834); II, 39 (to W. W. Hull, April 27, 1836).

30. Matthew Arnold, *Culture and Anarchy*, ed. J. Dover Wilson (Cambridge, Eng., 1966 [published serially in 1867–8 and as a volume in 1869]), p. 142.

31. Matthew Arnold, pp. 13–14.

32. Matthew Arnold, p. 38.

33. Matthew Arnold, "Heinrich Heine," *Cornhill Magazine*, Aug. 1863, in *Essays Literary and Critical* (London, 1907), p. 121.

34. George Eliot, *Daniel Deronda*, chap. 34. Two other chapters, 62 and 63, have epigraphs from Heine.

227
Ashworth

Heroines

1. aspora: A History of Anti-Semitis 167, 151.

2. Myth of the Jew," in *Speaking of Litera* 1980), p. 68. (This essay was written in 1930 or 1931 but not d until 1978 in *Commentary*.)

3. A. N. Wilson, *The Laird of Abbotsford: A View of Sir Walter Scott* (Oxford, 1980), p. 156.

4. Walter Scott, *Ivanhoe* (Penguin, London, 1986), pp. 405, 407.

5. *Ivanhoe*, p. 49.

6. *Ivanhoe*, pp. 521, 525.

7. *Ivanhoe*, p. 242.

8. *Ivanhoe*, p. 69.

9. *Ivanhoe*, p. 70.

10. *Ivanhoe*, p. 117.

11. *Ivanhoe*, p. 226.

12. *Ivanhoe*, pp. 246–7.

13. *Ivanhoe*, p. 201.

14. *Ivanhoe*, pp. 424–6.

15. *Ivanhoe*, pp. 435–6.

16. *Ivanhoe*, p. 518.

17. *Ivanhoe*, p. 300.

18. *Ivanhoe*, pp. 544–45.

19. *Ivanhoe*, p. 515.

20. Wilson, p. 156.

21. J. G. Lockhart, *Life of Sir Walter Scott* (New York, 1871), pp. 601–2; Tuchman, p. 81.

22. Quoted by Trilling, p. 73.

23. Benjamin Disraeli, *Coningsby, Or the New Generation* (Collected Works, Longmans, Green, London [n.d.]), pp. viii-ix.

24. *Coningsby*, pp. 209, 213, 220.

25. Disraeli, *Tancred, or the New Crusade* (Collected Works, Longmans, Green, London [n.d.] p. 149.

26. *Tancred*, p. 40.

27. *Tancred*, pp. 54–5.

28. *Tancred*, pp. 122–5.

29. Barbara Tuchman, *Bible and Sword: England and Palestine from the Bronze Age to Balfour* (New York, 1968), pp. 221–2.

30. *Tancred*, pp. 183–4. Some parts of the novel are almost straight historical narrative—e.g., pp. 344–50.

31. *Tancred*, p. 196.

32. *Tancred*, p. 262.

33. *Tancred*, p. 266.

34. *Tancred*, pp. 485–6.

35. See above, pp. 72–3.

36. *Tancred*, p. 427.

37. William Flavelle Monypenny and George Earle Buckle, *The Life of Benjamin Disraeli* (London, 1929), I, 864.

38. Benjamin Disraeli, *Lord George Bentinck: A Political Biography* (4th ed., London, 1852 [1st ed., 1851]), pp. 482–508.

39. Robert Blake, *Disraeli* (New York, 1966), pp. 260–61.

40. Blake, p. 191.

41. *The George Eliot Letters*, ed. Gordon S. Haight (New Haven, Conn., 1954–5, 1977–8), I, 246–7 (to John Sibree, Feb. 11, 1848). (Italics in original.)

42. *Eliot Letters*, IX, 282 (Edith Simcox's Autobiography).

43. *Daniel Deronda* (New York, 1961), p. 388.

44. *Daniel Deronda*, pp. 373–5.

45. *Daniel Deronda*, pp. 400, 402.

46. *Daniel Deronda*, p. 473.

47. *Daniel Deronda*, pp. 498–500.

48. *Daniel Deronda*, p. 606.

49. Gertrude Himmelfarb, *The Jewish Odyssey of George Eliot* (New York, 2009), pp. 137–40.

50. *Eliot Letters*, VI, 238 (Journal, April 12, 1876).

51. Edward W. Said, *The Question of Palestine* (New York, 1992 [1st ed., 1979]), pp. 63–6. For a survey and analysis of this "post-colonialist" critique of Eliot, see Nancy Henry, *George Eliot and the British Empire* (Cambridge, Eng., 2002).

52. F. R. Leavis, *The Great Tradition: George Eliot, Henry James, Joseph Conrad* (New York, 1948), pp. 79–125.

53. Walter Laqueur, *A History of Zionism* (New York, 1972), p. 101.

54. Shalom Goldman, *Zeal for Zion: Christians, Jews, and the Idea of the Promised Land* (Chapel Hill, N.C., 2009), p. 22.

55. Trilling, pp. 73–6.

56. *Daniel Deronda*, p. 284.

57. George Eliot, *Impressions of Theophrastus Such*, ed. Nancy Henry (Iowa City, 1994), pp. 146–52.

58. *Impressions*, pp. 162–4.

59. R. H. Horne defended Dickens against this charge in *A New Spirit of the Age* (New York, 1844), p. 18. See also Amy Cruse, *The Victorians and their Reading* (Boston, 1936), p. 152.

60. *The Girlhood of Queen Victoria: A Selection from Her Diaries, 1832–59*, ed. Harry Stone (Bloomington, Ind., 1968), I, 13 (March 30, 1850).

61. *The Letters of Charles Dickens*, ed. Madeline House, Graham Storey, and Kathleen Tillotson (Oxford, 1998), X, 269 (n. 6). (Eliza Davis to Dickens, June 22, 1863; Dickens's reply, July 10, 1863).

62. Dickens, *Our Mutual Friend* (New York, 1960), pp. 278ff.

63. Dickens *Letters*, X, 454 (n.1). (Davis to Dickens, Nov. 13, 1864; Dickens's reply, Nov. 16, 1864.)

64. Trilling, p. 71. An excellent study of this subject is the essay by Harry Stone, "Dickens and the Jews," *Victorian Studies*, March 1959. On this episode in particular see Edgar Johnson, "Dickens, Fagin, and Mr. Riah," *Commentary*, Jan. 1950.

65. Shirley Robin Letwin, *The Gentleman in Trollope: Individuality and Moral Conduct* (Cambridge, Mass., 1982), p. 74.

66. Anthony Trollope, *The Way We Live Now* (Oxford, 1951), II, 92–3, 277, 263, 362.

67. John Buchan, *The Thirty-Nine Steps* (Penguin ed., London, 1956), p. 17.

68. *Thirty-Nine Steps*, p. 46. I am among those who quoted and misinterpreted this passage as evidence of Buchan's antisemitism. ("John Buchan: An Untimely Appreciation," in *The Moral Imagination: From Edmund Burke to Lionel Trilling* [Chicago, 2006], p. 144.) The essay originally appeared in *Encounter*, Sept., 1960, and was criticized by some because it portrayed Buchan as an antisemite, and by others because it vindicated him on that charge. (My title, an "appreciation," suggests the latter.)

69. *Thirty-Nine Steps*, p. 90.

70. *Thirty-Nine Steps*, p. 13.

71. Janet Adam Smith, *John Buchan: A Biography* (London, 1965), p. 156.

72. Buchan, *The Three Hostages* (Penguin ed., London, 1953), pp. 17, 25.

73. Smith, pp. 316–17.

74. Private letter to me by a participant in the ceremonies.

75. Smith, p. 469.

V. From Evangelicalism to Zionism

1. See above, p. 119.

2. G. F. A. Best, *Shaftesbury* (London, 1964), p. 52. On Shaftesbury's political views, see above, chap. III.

3. Donald M. Lewis, *The Origins of Christian Zionism: Lord Shaftesbury and Evangelical Support for a Jewish Homeland* (Cambridge, Eng., 2010), pp. 117–18 (diary, July 30, 1826).

4. Text of the agenda in article on the London Society on the Internet.

5. Edwin Hodder, *The Life and Work of the Seventh Earl of Shaftesbury* (London, 1888), p. 123 (diary, Sept. 29, 1838).

6. William D. Rubinstein and Hilary L. Rubinstein, *Philosemitism: Admiration and Support in the English-Speaking World for Jews* (London, 1999), pp. 158–9 (quoting Shaftesbury, "State and Prospects of the Jews," *Quarterly Review*, Jan./Mar. 1839); and Hodder, pp. 126–7.

7. Hodder, p. 169 (letter to Palmerston, Sept. 25, 1840).

8. Hodder, p. 167 (diary, Aug. 1, 1840). Shaftesbury repeatedly referred to Jews as "God's [or "His" or "Thine"] ancient people." See also Donald Lewis, p. 147 (diary, Oct. 8, 1843); Hodder, 632 (letter to Gladstone, Dec. 22, 1868). The phrase appears in his diary as late as Feb. 2, 1882 (Hodder, p. 732).

9. Donald Lewis, p. 146 (letter to Princess Lieven, Nov. 13, 1840).

10. Barbara W. Tuchman, *Bible and Sword: England and Palestine from the Bronze Age to Balfour* (New York, 1968), p. 205 (diary, Nov. 12, 1841).

11. Hodder, p. 203 (diary, Nov. 18, 1841).

12. Hodder, p. 270 (diary, Aug. 27, 1843).

13. Hodder, p. 493 (italics in original) (diary, May 17, 1854).

14. Edward W. Said, *The Question of Palestine* (New York, 1979), p. 9. For a discussion of the dispute over the origin and meaning of this expression, see Adam Garfinkle, "On the Origin, Meaning, Use and Abuse of a Phrase," *Middle Eastern Studies*, Oct. 1991; and Diana Muir, "A Land Without a People for a People Without a Land," *Middle East Quarterly*, Spring 2008.

15. Donald Lewis, p. 319 (speech to the Palestine Exploration Fund Society, 1875).

16. Quoted by Tuchman, p. 251.

17. Best, p. 126.

18. Hodder, p. 737.

19. Theodor Herzl, *The Jewish State*, tr. Sylvie D'Avigdore (reproduced on the Internet, p. 18). Herzl probably started the book before the Dreyfus affair, but it was surely in his mind as he wrote it. Geoffrey Lewis points out that there is no mention of Dreyfus in Herzl's diaries. (*Balfour and Weizmann: The Zionist, the Zealot and the Emergence of Israel* [London, 2009], p. 12).

20. Geoffrey Lewis, p. 37.

21. Walter Laqueur, *A History of Zionism* (New York, 1972), p. 112.

22. Yoram Hazony, *The Jewish State: The Struggle for Israel's Soul* (New York, 2000), p. 164.

23. *Encyclopaedia Judaica* (Jerusalem, 1972), IV, 131 (a reproduction of the letter).

24. Jonathan Schneer, *The Balfour Declaration: The Origins of the Arab-Israel Conflicty* (New York, 2010), is a detailed account of the "contradictions, deceptions, misinterpretations, and wishful

thinking" that led to the Declaration, which "produced a murderous harvest . . . [that] we go on harvesting even today" (368). The emphasis throughout is on the "deceit," "intrigue," and "double-dealing" (xxix) that were, as the sub-title put it, "the origins of the Arab-Israel conflict." My emphasis is on the ideas and visions (and, yes, contradictions and deceptions) that led to the Declaration, and on the Declaration itself, for all its faults and ambiguities, as the historic origin of the state of Israel.

25. Donald Lewis, p. 333.

26. Blanche E. C. Dugdale, *Arthur James Balfour* (New York, 1937), I, 324.

27. Tuchman, p. 312.

28. Geoffrey Lewis, p. 63.

29. Michael Makovsky, *Churchill's Promised Land: Zionism and Statecraft* (New Haven, Conn., 2007), p. 77.

30. A. J. Balfour, *Essays Speculative and Political* (London, 1920), pp. 259–60.

31. Balfour, *Essays*, p. 266.

32. Balfour, *Essays*, pp. 261–2.

33. Balfour, speech in the House of Lords, June 21, 1922. (All the parliamentary speeches cited in this chapter are from Hansard's Parliamentary Debates, reproduced on the Internet.)

34. Dugdale, II, 235, 409.

35. John Maynard Keynes, *Essays in Biography* (London, 1951 [1st ed., 1933]), pp. 35–6.

36. Rubinstein, p. 167.

37. Martin Gilbert, *Churchill and the Jews: A Lifelong Friendship* (New York, 2007), p. 24.

38. Tuchman, p. 336.

39. Tuchman, p. 323.

40. Tuchman, p. 323.

41. Rubinstein, p. 145.

42. Rubinstein, p. 168.

43. Rubinstein, p. 168.

44. Roy Jenkins, *Churchill* (London, 2001), p. 108. (Not quite "exactly"; the Aliens Act was passed in 1905, the election was in 1906.)

45. Makovsky, p. 62 (quoting the *Jewish Chronicle*, Feb. 7, 1908) (italics in original).

46. Churchill, "Zionism versus Bolshevism: A Struggle for the Soul of the Jewish People," *Illustrated Sunday Herald*, February 8, 1920. The Disraeli quotation early in the article was cited often by Churchill in different contexts and sometimes slightly differently worded. Historians have not found the "well-known occasion" when Disraeli made that pronouncement, although it certainly represents his views.

47. Gilbert, pp. 56–7.

48. Makovsky, p. 235. Churchill took credit for coining this phrase, but it was Herbert Samuel who suggested the concept and drafted the White Paper.

49. Gilbert, p. 85; Makovsky, p. 132.

50. Makovsky, p. 146.

51. Makovsky, p. 150.

52. Churchill, speech in the House of Commons, May 23, 1939.

53. Gilbert, p. 161.

54. Anthony Julius, *Trials of the Diaspora: A History of Anti-Semitism in England* (Oxford, 2010), p. 323 (letter to Lord Cranborne, July 1942).

55. Makovsky, p. 191.

56. Churchill, speech in the House of Commons, Jan. 26, 1949. That "event in world history" echoed his essay about Jews and Bolshevism almost thirty years earlier. See above, pp. 139–140.

57. Gilbert, p. 279.

58. Gilbert, p. 295 (April 16, 1956).

59. Winston Churchill, *The Second World War: Closing the Ring* (Boston, 1953), V, 533.

60. William Manchester, *The Last Lion: Winston Spencer Churchill, Visions of Glory, 1874–1932* (New York, 1983), p. 177.

61. Gertrude Himmelfarb, *The Roads to Modernity: The British, French, and American Enlightenments* (New York, 2004), pp. 38–39 and endnotes 48 and 49, p. 246.

62. Winston Churchill, "Moses: The Leader of a People," *Sunday Chronicle*, Nov. 8, 1931, in Churchill, *Thoughts and Adventures* (New York, 1990), pp. 212–15.

63. Churchill, "Moses," p. 209.

64. Review by Piers Brendon of Martin Gilbert, *Churchill and the Jews*, in *The Independent*, July 13, 2007.

Epilogue

1. See above, p. 109.

2. See above, p. 8.

3. See above, pp. 141–2.

4. See above, pp. 75, 139.

5. Milton Himmelfarb, "What Do I Believe," *Commentary*, August 1996, reprinted in *Jews and Gentiles*, ed. Gertrude Himmelfarb (New York, 2007), p. 163. See also *The Politics of Hope* (London, 1997) by Jonathan Sacks, the Chief Rabbi of Great Britain.

Index